Essent~

CON ~ACT LAW

Essential Cases

CONTRACT LAW

Tikus Little, LL.B. (Hons), Dip.L.P.
Senior Teaching Fellow,
University of Stirling

DUNDEE UNIVERSITY PRESS
2012

Published in Great Britain in 2012 by
Dundee University Press
University of Dundee
Dundee DD1 4HN

www.dundee.ac.uk/dup

ISBN 978–1–84586–126–1

No natural forests were destroyed to make this product;
only farmed timber was used and replanted

British Library Cataloguing-in-Publication data
A catalogue for this book is available on request from the British Library.

Typeset by Koinonia, Bury
Printed and bound by CPI Group (UK) Ltd, Croydon, CR0 4YY

CONTENTS

General Principles

Formation of Contract

Problems with Contracts

(i) Lack of Consensus

(ii) Lack of Consent

Contractual Terms

TABLE OF CASES

Page references in **bold** type indicate those where the facts of the case are considered in the text.

GENERAL PRINCIPLES

Morton's Trustees v *Aged Christian Friend Society of Scotland*
(1899) 2 F 82

Court: Inner House, Court of Session

Issue: Can offers of charitable donations which are accepted be enforced?

Facts: Mr Morton made offers of donations to the Society which it accepted and most of which he paid. However, he died before all of the payments were made and the trustees of his estate argued that they were not bound to make the outstanding donations.

Judgment: Lord Kinnear found at p 221 that "[i]t is a familiar doctrine in the law of Scotland, differing in that respect from the law of England, that an obligation is binding although it may not proceed on a valuable consideration, or may not be expressed in a solemn form, such as a deed under seal. What is necessary is that the promissor should intend to bind himself by an enforceable obligation, and should express that intention in clear words".

The letters making the offers were clear and specific, with Mr Morton undertaking to pay if the Society was set up and run in a particular way and, as a result, the offers made in them and accepted were binding against successors.

Analysis: it is possible to have a contract in which the obligations appear to be one sided. In this case, Mr Morton did not benefit personally from the contracts but clearly obligated himself to pay if certain conditions were met.

Stone v MacDonald 1979 SC 363

Court: Outer House, Court of Session

Issue: Was an option to purchase contractual or a promise?

Facts: A landowner sold land to a farmer but included an option to purchase 3 acres of it within the following 10-year period, binding on their respective successors. Within that period, the landowner's successors wrote a letter which they claimed exercised that option.

The defenders, the farmer's successors, disputed that this letter was a proper exercise of the option.

Claim: The claim was by the landowner's successors for a declarator that the option had been exercised correctly and for delivery of a disposition (conveyance to transfer title) of the affected land. The defenders argued that because the option was about an interest in heritable property, it had to be exercised using formal writing which was not done. Accordingly, it was not valid and not binding.

Decision: Lord Ross agreed with the landowner's successors – the option had been exercised correctly because it did not require formal writing and so the 3 acres in question should be conveyed to them.

Judgment: Lord Ross agreed with prior authorities that the *exercise* of an option to purchase did not require probative writing. Although this case pre-dates the Requirements of Writing (Scotland) Act 1995, the common law required certain contracts to be in writing (these were known as *obligationes literis*). The defenders had argued that the option constituted an offer which required formal acceptance but Lord Ross said: "In my opinion, the better view is expressed by Lord Keith in *Sichi* v. *Biagi*, [1946 S.N. 66] *supra*. 'This in my opinion, is a case where on a sound construction of the document there arises a promise, as distinct from an offer.'"

Analysis: An option can be categorised as a promise (this will depend on its wording, of course).

Littlejohn v Hadwen (1882) 20 SLR 5

Court: Court of Session

Issue: Was a promise to keep an offer open for a certain period enforceable as a promise?

Facts: A offered to sell land to B and to keep the offer open for a period of time but then reneged on that.

Claim: B claimed that the offer to keep the offer open was a promise and enforceable as such.

Decision: The court agreed and the offer to keep it open was a promise enforceable in law.

Judgment: The judgment was summarised neatly in the House of Lords case of *A & G Paterson* v *Highland Railway Co* 1927 SC (HL) 32 by Viscount Dunedin at p 38: "I am prepared to say that the opinion of Lord Ordinary Fraser, expressed in the now old case of *Littlejohn v Hadwen* in which I was counsel many years ago, is right, *i.e.*, if I offer my property to a certain person at a certain price, and go on to say: 'This offer is to be open up to a certain date', I cannot withdraw that offer before that date, if the person to whom I made the offer chooses to accept it. It would be different in England, for in the case supposed there would be no consideration for the promise to keep the offer open. But what is the reason of this? It is because the offer as made contained two distinct promises: (1) to sell at a certain price, and (2) to keep the offer open."

Analysis: This is a good example of a unilateral gratuitous obligation (also known as promise) in Scots law. Note Viscount Dunedin's assessment in a later case that it would be decided differently in England because of the doctrine of consideration applicable there.

Bathgate v *Rosie* 1976 SLT (Sh Ct) 16

Court: Sheriff court

Issue: Was a mother's promise to pay for a broken window enforceable?

Facts: Mrs Rosie's son broke a window and she promised to pay for the damage. However, when presented with the bill, she refused to pay.

Claim: Mr Bathgate argued that the promise was enforceable and raised an action for payment against the child's parents. They claimed that the promise had been made in error as the mother thought she was legally liable.

Decision: The sheriff rejected the error argument and found in fact that the promise had been made voluntarily and because Mrs Rosie did not want her husband to find out about the broken window.

Judgment: The sheriff found (at pp 17 and 18) that "It was not disputed that, in that event, the second-named defender gave an undertaking which although gratuitous is recognised as binding by the law of Scotland, and from which she can escape only if she established that she gave it because her mind was affected by some error."

Analysis: This case is an example of a promise being enforced and it reiterates that gratuitous obligations can be legally binding.

Petrie v *Earl of Airlie* (1834) 13 S 68

Court: Inner House, Court of Session

Issue: Enforceability of promise to pay a reward.

Facts: During a campaign surrounding voting reforms, the Earl of Airlie offered a reward for information leading to the detection and conviction of those responsible for publishing certain placards which named him as someone who had voted against reform in a meeting. Mr Petrie duly reported his brother and another man but no prosecution came of it. The Earl refused to pay out.

Claim: Mr Petrie claimed his reward.

Decision: The court held in favour of Mr Petrie.

Judgment: The Earl had been mistaken about whether a prosecution and conviction could actually take place on the grounds alleged, but that was his own mistake. The promise to pay the reward stood.

Analysis: This case is authority for the point that a promise to pay a reward can be enforceable in law.

Carlill v *Carbolic Smokeball Co* [1893] 1 QB 256

Court: Court of Appeal (English case)

Issue: Could a contract be concluded on the basis of a public advertisement followed by action on the part of a member of the public? Was the advert an "offer" capable of acceptance?

Facts: The Carbolic Smokeball Co placed adverts in papers as follows: "100l. reward will be paid by the Carbolic Smoke Ball Company to any person who contracts the increasing epidemic influenza, colds, or any disease caused by taking cold, after having used the ball three times daily for two weeks according to the printed directions supplied with each ball. 1000l. is deposited with the Alliance Bank, Regent Street, shewing our sincerity in the matter.

During the last epidemic of influenza many thousand carbolic smoke balls were sold as preventives against this disease, and in no ascertained case was the disease contracted by those using the carbolic smoke ball.

One carbolic smoke ball will last a family several months, making it the cheapest remedy in the world at the price, 10s., post free. The ball can be refilled at a cost of 5s. Address, Carbolic Smoke Ball

Company, 27, Princes Street, Hanover Square, London."

Mrs Carlill bought one, used it as instructed but still caught flu. She claimed the £100.

Claim: Mrs Carlill, the plaintiff, claimed that the advert was an offer and that her actions in purchasing the ball and using it constituted an acceptance. There was therefore a contract which she was entitled to enforce. This was disputed by the defendant, the Carbolic Smokeball Co, which claimed that the advert was "merely an expression of intention" and that the contract could not be concluded by the "private act" of Mrs Carlill: it was simply a "puff".

Decision: There was an enforceable contract.

Judgment: In a unanimous judgment, the three judges held that an offer could be made to the world at large and that a contract would result from an individual then accepting that offer using the method of acceptance stipulated which in this case was the purchase and correct use of the ball. Lord Linley wrote at p 270: "… how are we to find out whether the person who makes the offer does intimate that notification of acceptance will not be necessary in order to constitute a binding bargain? In many cases you look to the offer itself. In many cases you extract from the character of the transaction that notification is not required, and in the advertisement cases it seems to me to follow as an inference to be drawn from the transaction itself that a person is not to notify his acceptance of the offer before he performs the condition, but that if he performs the condition notification is dispensed with. It seems to me that from the point of view of common sense no other idea could be entertained".

Analysis: This English decision talks about promise and bargains almost interchangeably but the key point to take from it is that it is persuasive English authority that an offer made to the public at large and not to a designated person is still a valid offer capable of acceptance and that the acceptance may be by private action if that is the method of acceptance to be inferred from the offer itself. The later Scottish case of *Hunter* v *General Accident, Fire and Life Assurance Corp* 1909 SC (HL) 30 confirmed the Scots law position that an advert to the public at large could be an offer (although in that case different stipulations about acceptance were given in the advert).

FORMATION OF CONTRACT

Fisher v *Bell* [1960] 1 QB 394

Court: Divisional Court (English case)

Issue: Was a shop display including a flick knife an offer to sell under the Restriction of Offensive Weapons Act 1959 or an invitation to treat?

Facts: A policeman spotted a flick knife in a shop window soon after this Act was passed. There was a price ticket behind it. At the time, s 1(1) of the Act stated:

> "(1) Any person who manufactures, sells or hires or offers for sale or hire, or lends to gives to any other person—
>
> > (a) any knife which has a blade which opens automatically by hand pressure applied to a button, spring or other device in or attached to the handle of the knife, sometimes known as a 'flick knife' or 'flick gun';…
>
> shall be guilty of an offence."

Claim: The prosecution was of the opinion that this was an offer to sell in terms of the Act and therefore a criminal offence. However, the defendant's counsel argued that this was not an offer but was "mere possession" even if the knives were in the shop window.

Decision: The Act did not define "offer to sell" and so the ordinary law of contract had to be applied. The ordinary law of contract is that a shop display is an invitation to treat and not an offer.

Judgment: Lord Parker CJ said: "It is perfectly clear that according to the ordinary law of contract the display of an article with a price on it in a shop window is merely an invitation to treat. It is in no sense an offer for sale the acceptance of which constitutes a contract. That is clearly the general law of the country."

Analysis: This case confirms that shop displays are not offers in terms of the law of contract. Soon after this case, a new Act was passed (Restriction of Offensive Weapons Act 1961) which amended the 1959 Act to include "possession for the purpose of sale or hire" under the list of offences. It is accepted that Scots law would follow the same line and the fact that it has not been brought to the Scottish courts suggests that this position is accepted here and that a test case has not been found necessary.

Pharmaceutical Society of Great Britain v *Boots Cash Chemists (Southern) Ltd* [1952] 2 QB 795

Court: Queen's Bench Division (English case)

Issue: Did Boots contravene the Pharmacy and Poisons Act 1933 by "offering" drugs for sale on self-service display shelves?

Facts: Self-service shops are the norm now but when first introduced, they posed some legal questions. In this case, Boots had displayed certain drugs on the self-service shelves which customers then had to take to the checkout in order to pay for them. These drugs included some which could only be sold "by" or "under the supervision of" a pharmacist. The procedure was that the customer would take the drugs to the checkout and the cashier would then alert the on-duty pharmacist who would authorise the purchase (or not).

Claim: The plaintiffs argued that Boots was breaching the law because this method could not be said to be a sale by or under the supervision of a pharmacist. They argued that *Carlill* v *Carbolic Smokeball Co* should be interpreted to apply to this display: according to their argument, the display was therefore an offer and the contract was concluded when the customer accepted it by picking up the goods and taking them to the cashier, ie the pharmacist's role came too late in the contractual process to comply with the law on drugs and poisons.

Decision: The court held that the display was an invitation to treat, not an offer, and accepted the defendants' claim that display on self-service shelves is no different to displays in shop cabinets or windows.

Judgment: Lord Goddard CJ said at p 800: "The question which I have to decide is whether the sale is completed before or after the intending purchaser has passed the scrutiny of the pharmacist and paid his money, or, to put it in another way, whether the offer which initiates the negotiations is an offer by the shopkeeper or an offer by the buyer." He went on to say: "I think that it is a well-established principle that the mere exposure of goods for sale by a shopkeeper indicates to the public that he is willing to treat but does not amount to an offer to sell. I do not think I ought to hold that that principle is completely reversed merely because there is a self-service scheme, such as this, in operation. In my opinion it comes to no more than that the customer is informed that he may himself pick up an article and bring it to the shopkeeper with a view to buying it, and if, but only if, the shopkeeper then expresses his willingness to sell, the contract for sale is completed."

Analysis: This persuasive English authority tells us that shop displays in self-service shops are an invitation to treat, not an offer. Old law was applied to a novel situation.

Partridge v *Crittenden* [1968] 1 WLR 1204

Court: Queen's Bench Division (English case)

Issue: Was a newspaper advert in which the type and price of a bird were given an offer to sell or an invitation to treat?

Facts: Mr Partridge placed an advert in a newspaper which stated: "Quality British A.B.C.R. ... bramblefinch cocks, bramblefinch hens ... 25s each" and someone sent him the money and asked for a hen which he duly sent. The RSPCA brought a prosecution against him on the basis that he had "offered for sale" a bird in contravention of the Protection of Birds Act 1954: the Act allowed the sale of "closed ring" birds bred in captivity but, in this case, the ring around the bird's leg could be removed without injury, implying that it had not been bred in captivity and thus the offer for sale was a breach of the Act.

Claim: The RSPCA's claim centred on the terms of the Act and the definition of "closed ring" but the appellant's case was that (1) there had been no offer to sell, merely an invitation to treat; and (2) the issues around the ring were disputed.

Decision: The newspaper advert was not an offer to sell but an invitation to treat and as there was no offer, there was no offence under the Act.

Judgment: Ashworth J said at p 1208: "... the real point of substance in this case arose from the words 'offer for sale' and it is to be noted in section 6 of the Act of 1954 that the operative words are 'any person sells, offers for sale or has in his possession for sale.'" His Lordship cited the case of *Fisher* v *Bell* and said: "The words are the same here 'offer for sale', and in my judgment the law of the country is equally plain as it was in regard to articles in a shop window, namely that the insertion of an advertisement in the form adopted here under the title 'Classified Advertisements' is simply an invitation to treat."

Analysis: Another English case but persuasive authority for the point that adverts are usually classed as invitations to treat.

Hunter v *General Accident, Fire and Life Assurance Corp*
1909 SC (HL) 30

Court: House of Lords (Scottish case)

Issue: The case centres on the interpretation and application of terms in a contract of insurance but also concerns the validity of an offer made to the public at large.

Facts: Mr Hunter bought a Letts diary which contained a coupon stating "One thousand pounds will be paid under the following conditions by the above Corporation to the heirs, executors, or administrators of any person killed solely and directly by bodily injuries received in … railway travelling … or who shall have been fatally injured thereby, should death result within three calendar months after such accident … Provided that at the time of such accident the person so killed or injured was the owner of the publication in which this insurance coupon is inserted, that such person had duly caused his or her name to be registered at the Head Office of the Corporation in Perth, and had paid the fee for registration and cost of acknowledgment, and that notice of claim is sent to the registered office of the Corporation at Perth within fourteen days of the occurrence of the accident, *and that such claim be made within twelve months of the registration of the holder's name.*"

On 25 December 1905 Mr Hunter had sent in the form of application for registration, which was processed by the insurance company. He was involved in a railway accident on 28 December 1906, dying the following day. His widow intimated a claim on the insurance policy on 2 January 1907. The issue was: if the claim had to be made within 12 months of the date of registration, what was the "date of registration"?

Claim: The insurance company claimed that the contract had been formed by Mr Hunter's acceptance of the publicly made offer in the diary and that the acceptance was received by it on 27 December (or, at latest, it took effect on the 29th when it was itself acknowledged). The insurers argued that this was the date from which the 12-month period should run. Mr Hunter's widow, as executrix, argued that since the 12 months ran from date of registration, not the date of the contract, the date of *registration* was not completed until 3 January 1906 when the form was dated, filed and intimated to Mr Hunter and the claim was therefore within the 12-month time limit.

Judgment: The Lord President observed at p 658 that "the contract here was undoubtedly made by the sending of the deceased's communication to the insurance company; in other words, I think that the communication embodied in the coupon is an open offer which is made into a contract by acceptance, and that it does not require a further acceptance on the part of the Company".

Analysis: Although the outcome of this case hinged on the interpretation of "date of registration", it also confirms that an offer can be made to the public in Scots law.

Philp & Co v *Knoblauch* 1907 SC 994

Court: Inner House, Court of Session

Issue: Offer or quotation/tender?

Facts: Knoblauch was an agent who sent a letter to Philp & Co saying:

> "Dear Sirs,—I am offering to-day Plate Linseed for January/ February shipment to Leith, and have pleasure in quoting you 100 tons at 41/3, usual Plate terms. I shall be glad to hear if you are buyers, and await your esteemed reply.— Yours truly, Hugo Knoblauch."

Philp & Co accepted those terms and thought that they had a contract but Knoblauch said that this had not been an offer and there was no contract. Linseed prices fluctuated and so by the time Philp & Co bought 100 tons from another supplier, they had to pay more for it. Philp & Co sued Knoblauch for the difference in price.

Claim: Philp & Co claimed that there was a contract which had been breached but Knoblauch's position was that there had been no offer and no contract. The Lord Ordinary in the Outer House decided that there was indeed no offer so Philp & Co appealed to the Inner House.

Judgment: The court found in favour of Philp & Co. The Lord Justice-Clerk said: "This first letter … is not a letter merely indicating that the defender had certain goods at his disposal and would be glad to enter into negotiations with regard to them, but stated that he had 'pleasure in quoting you (the pursuers) 100 tons (of linseed) at 41/3 usual Plate terms', and that he awaited 'your esteemed reply'. That, I think, was clearly an offer of the 100 tons at a named price." The case of *Harvey* v *Facey* which had been cited by the defender, Knoblauch, was correct but did not apply to this case which was *in re mercatoria* (ie a business situation) and not a heritable property case.

Analysis: This case is a good example of a situation in business where parties are used to corresponding in shorthand and, although based on telegrams, the decision would be equally applicable to an e-mail case today.

Camarthen Developments Ltd v *Pennington* [2008] CSOH 139

Court: Outer House, Court of Session

Issue: When was a notice purifying conditions in missives effective? Did the postal rule apply to such a notice?

Facts: A contract for the sale of land was concluded (such contracts are called "missives") in which an option was granted in favour of the purchaser to waive certain conditions which had been included in the contract. The conditions concerned planning permission, a survey and satisfaction as to services. If the conditions were purified (ie fulfilled) or waived, the seller would be due additional payments. If the purchaser did not purify or waive the conditions within the set time period, the seller could resile from the missives (ie withdraw without penalty). The missives set out how notice of purification or waiver was to be effected. Even although the purchasers obtained the planning permission etc that they needed, the deadline approached without notices being received and so the seller decided to exercise his right to resile. On Saturday, 20 October 2007 he had his solicitor send a fax resiling, which fax became effective as a notice in terms of the missives at 9 am on the Monday morning (ie 22 October). In the meantime, the purchaser's solicitors had put a letter enclosing notices of purification in the post at 5.55 pm on Friday, 19 October, which notices were in the mail bag which the seller's solicitor collected from Jedburgh Post Office at 8.50 am on Monday, 22 October. He arrived at his office with the bag at 9.03 am.

Claim: The purchasers argued that they had purified the conditions (and thus removed the seller's right to resile) before the notice to resile took effect at 9am on Monday 22 October. They put forward three reasons: (1) the postal rule should be applied so that purification took effect at 5.55 pm on Friday; or (2) on the balance of probabilities, the notices of purification arrived in Jedburgh on the Saturday morning and so took effect then; or (3) the latest time they took effect was when the seller's solicitor collected the mail bag at 8.50 on the Monday morning. Thus, the seller could not resile and the contract stood.

Decision: The notices of purification were held to have been served effectively at 8.50 am on the Monday morning when the mail bag was collected by the seller's solicitor, thus beating the notice resiling from the missives by 10 minutes. The contract stood.

Judgment: Lord Hodge, at para 14, held: "I am not persuaded that there is any rule in Scots law that the posting of a letter exercising an option falls to be treated as the acceptance of an offer. While an option contract is very similar in effect to a unilateral promise to keep an offer open for acceptance for a specified period, the exercise of an option is not the acceptance of an offer but the exercise of a contractual right conferred by the option agreement" before going on to state "There may be disagreement as to the correct legal characterisation of an option in Scots law, namely whether it is a unilateral promise by the grantor, a conditional contract of sale or *sui generis* (for the various characterisations in English law see Chitty, para 3.170, fn 870). Different forms of option agreement may lend themselves more readily to one or other characterisation. Indeed, some agreements which have been described as options may amount only to an offer to sell and not constitute an option agreement (viz. Lord Ross in *Stone and Another* v *MacDonald* 1979 SLT 288 , at p 291 where he discusses *Hamilton* v *Lochrane* (1899) 1 F 478). Whatever the particular characterisation, most arrangements which are described as options have certain effects. First, until the party to whom the option has been granted intimates his intention to exercise the option, he is under no obligation to purchase the option subjects. Secondly, once a contract or unilateral promise has created the option, the exercise of that option is the exercise of the right conferred by that contract or promise and not the acceptance of an offer. Thirdly, when the party in whose favour the option has been given intimates the exercise of that right he becomes bound to complete the contract by purchasing the subjects. Thus while the exercise of the option by the grantee brings into being bilateral obligations, that effect does not make the exercise of the option the acceptance of an offer. It would therefore be a significant extension of the postal acceptance rule to hold that an option was exercised on the posting of a letter rather than on the communication of the exercise of the option by the grantor's receipt of the letter."

Analysis: This is an interesting case about the timing of notices and of interest in the area of offer and acceptance because of the discussion about the applicability of the postal rule to the exercise of options. The postal rule stays firmly in the zone of "offers" and not "options".

Wylie & Lochhead v *McElroy & Sons* (1873) 1 R 41

Court: Inner House, Court of Session

Issue: Can an offer lapse if not accepted in a "reasonable time"?

Facts: McElroy & Sons offered to carry out certain iron works for Wylie & Lochhead at a certain price and this was not accepted until 5 weeks later (with a variation of terms).

Claim: Wylie & Lochhead wanted to proceed with the contract on the price quoted in the offer but McElroy & Sons claimed that its original offer had fallen because it had not been accepted in a reasonable time. This was very important because prices for metal and similar commodities can fluctuate quite wildly in short periods of time and the original price was no longer viable for them.

Decision: The court agreed with McElroy & Sons and the offer had lapsed.

Judgment: The definition of "reasonable time" will vary depending on the circumstances. Here, the price of iron fluctuated considerably and the court was entitled to look at the commercial context within which the offer was made.

Analysis: Offers do not remain open indefinitely. Some may have a time limit for acceptance written into them but if they do not then they will lapse if not accepted in a "reasonable time". The court will look at the commercial context of the contract to determine that length of time.

Wolf and Wolf v *Forfar Potato Co* 1984 SLT 100

Court: Inner House, Court of Session

Issue: Effect of a counter-offer or a qualified acceptance on an offer.

Facts: Potato merchants from Forfar made an offer to sell potatoes to an international potato merchant. The merchant accepted the offer but included some new conditions in the acceptance (ie conditions which had not formed part of the original offer). They made a phone call to discuss matters further and sent a further telex, asking that these conditions be considered. The Forfar merchants did not supply the potatoes and were sued for damages for breach of contract.

Claim: The international merchant claimed that a valid contract had been concluded but this was disputed by the Forfar merchant who said that there was no *consensus in idem* and so no contract. The case was taken to the sheriff court first and the sheriff found in favour of the Forfar merchant: no contract and no loss anyway. The international merchant appealed the case to the Court of Session.

Judgment: The court applied the principle set out in Gloag, who, under reference to *Hunter* v *Hunters* and *Hyde* v *Wrench*, says at p 37: "An offer falls if it is refused. If the refusal is not peremptory, but combined with a request for better terms, the general construction is that the offer is gone, and that the party to whom it was made, on failure to obtain the terms he requests, cannot fall back on an acceptance of the original offer" (Lord Justice-Clerk (Lord Wheatley) quoting Gloag at p 103).

Although Lord McDonald doubted the authorities used by Gloag, all three judges in the present case supported the basic point of law. Thus, the reply to the original offer was a counter-offer and cancelled out the original offer. It would have taken acceptance of the international merchant's terms by the Forfar merchant to conclude the contract and, despite the telephone call and the subsequent telex, this had not happened as a matter of fact and so as a matter of law there was no concluded contract.

Analysis: If the reply to an offer contains additional conditions, it may be a counter-offer or qualified acceptance which then requires an additional step of acceptance by the original offeror to conclude the contract. The original offer is no longer open for a straight acceptance either.

Jacobsen, Sons & Co v *E Underwood & Son Ltd* (1894) 21 R 654

Court: Second Division, Court of Session

Issue: The postal rule – whether the fact that a letter of acceptance was incorrectly addressed impacted on the application of the postal rule.

Facts: The defenders made an offer to buy goods and put an acceptance date on it. The pursuers wrote to accept that offer and posted it on the day for acceptance. However, the letter was not addressed correctly and it was slightly delayed in reaching the purchasers who then refused to accept the delivery when it followed.

Claim: The sellers claimed damages, being the difference between the price of the goods in the offer and the amount they managed to get on "re-sale". The defenders, as purchasers, argued that there was no concluded contract.

Judgment: The postal rule is clear that posting the acceptance concludes the contract – the act of posting is the act of acceptance. The fact that the letter was incorrectly addressed (missing out the seller's street name and number) did not alter this fact because the same format of addressing letters had been sent in the past with no delays.

Analysis: The postal rule is quite straightforward and this case looks like an attempt to get out of the contract on a "technicality" by the purchasers since the mode of address of letters was well established in a commercial relationship between the two parties. Of course, a blank envelope might have had a different outcome!

Uniroyal v *Miller & Co* 1985 SLT 101

Court: Outer House, Court of Session

Issue: Which conditions applied in a contract concluded in a "battle of forms"?

Facts: Two court actions were referred to in this opinion on the preliminary issue of what the contractual terms to be applied actually were before moving on to consider the alleged breach of contract: one which the court referred to as the "1974 action" and the other as the "1976 action".

Facts for the 1974 action: the defenders, Miller & Co, sent a quotation for their products to Uniroyal's predecessor in this contract,

Rubber Regenerating, on their standard form which had their conditions of contract on the back. In response, Rubber Regenerating sent a purchase order to them and this purchase order had *their* conditions printed on the back which were different and, indeed, sought to exclude the sellers' terms. Miller & Co sent a written acknowledgement with a price change and the statement that the acceptance was "subject to the conditions printed on the back of this form".

Facts for the 1976 action: again, the defenders gave a written quotation to Uniroyal, with conditions on the reverse, and the pursuers telephoned to place an order but there was some disagreement about the specification of the products at that time. However, Miller & Co sent a written acknowledgement of the "order", again with their terms on the reverse. Uniroyal sent a telex (early version of the fax) the next day, confirming the order, followed by a letter a couple of days after that.

Claim: Uniroyal sued Miller & Co for breach of contract. The effect of and consequence of breach depended on the terms of the contracts. Miller & Co argued that their conditions prevailed and these excluded the consequential damages which Uniroyal were seeking. Uniroyal disagreed

Decision: The defenders' terms applied.

Judgment: Lord Allanbridge said: "Apart from the difference of approach to 'the battle of the forms', adopted on the one hand by Lord Denning and on the other hand by Lawton and Bridge L.JJ. in the 1972 case of *Butler Machine Tool Co. Ltd.* v *Ex-Cell-O Corporation (England)* in the Court of Appeal, there was little real dispute between counsel on the principles of contract law to be applied in this case. It was the application of the facts in these two cases to these principles that caused the dissent between the parties ... The fundamental principle to be applied ... is to consider whether or not, and when, there has been consensus ad idem between the parties."

His Lordship opined that the law was correctly stated in Gloag on *Contract* (2nd edn) at p 39: "When the construction of a reply to an offer is in question, the difficulty has been to distinguish between an actual, though perhaps hesitating and reluctant, acceptance, and an offer to accept if the offerer is prepared to alter his terms. In the former case the contract is complete; in the latter the reply is in effect a new offer, and there is no contract unless the original offerer accedes to it. There is another possibility. What is put forward as an acceptance may be read as a mere expression of willingness to contract and of expectation that terms will be arranged."

His Lordship found that, in the 1974 case, the acknowledgement of order was actually a counter-offer because the price had not been agreed before then and price was essential to this particular contract: there could not be *consensus in idem* until the price had been agreed here. This counter-offer "killed off" the purchase order and, hence, the pursuers' terms on the back of it.

As for the 1976 case, the court found that the telephone order was an acceptance of the offer and so the defenders' terms also applied to this contract. This was despite the fact that the exact specification of the products was still being thrashed out at that stage. There was sufficient *consensus in idem* at that point to conclude the contract, subject to a few details being agreed.

Analysis: In a battle of the forms (ie where standard terms are printed on order forms, quotations, letters, acknowledgements etc), the court will examine the process to establish when *consensus in idem* has been reached and will deem the contract concluded at that point. However the parties label their letters, forms etc is not the point: the law will decide and the last set of conditions to be accepted wins. The English case of *Butler Machine Tool Co Ltd* v *Ex-Cell-O Corp* was followed in Scots law.

Continental Tyre & Rubber Co Ltd v *Trunk Trailer Co Ltd*
1985 SC 163, 1987 SLT 58

Court: Inner House, Court of Session

Issue: Was an exclusion of liability incorporated into a contract in which two sets of standard terms competed? Which terms were incorporated into the contract?

Facts: The defenders ordered tyres using their standard purchase form with conditions printed on it. The tyres were delivered by the pursuers in batches and, in each case, a delivery note with their terms and conditions was signed off by the defenders. However, they did not pay for them in full. In the meantime, the tyres were sold on but customers complained that they were not of "merchantable quality" under the Sale of Goods Act 1979 (since amended to "satisfactory quality"). When the tyre sellers claimed the balance of payment, the purchasers claimed "set-off" since the tyres were not of an acceptable quality and they had lost out to their customers as a result.

Claim: The pursuers claimed for the outstanding price and argued that even if the tyres were not of merchantable quality (which they denied), their terms and conditions excluded liability for that. Their terms and conditions were in their delivery note which they argued was contractual – a counter-offer to the purchase order which was accepted by the defenders' signature.

Decision: The delivery note was not contractual so the pursuers' terms and conditions were not effectively incorporated into the contract. It had been concluded before that point.

Judgment: Lord Emslie (Lord President) said at p 170 (SC) that: "The particular question in this case might be: were the pursuers reasonably entitled to conclude, in light of the conduct of the parties throughout their prior course of dealing, that the defenders ordered and received the tyres with which the action is concerned, accepting that the tyres were supplied subject to the terms of the pursuers' conditions of sale, including [the exclusion of warranty]? Putting the matter in another way, must the defenders, in all the circumstances of the prior communings in this case, be taken to have assented to the incorporation of these conditions of sale into this particular contract?" He thought not.

Analysis: The delivery note in this case was deemed post contractual so the terms in it were not incorporated and the pursuers did not have the protection of their terms which would have shielded them from the defenders' claims.

PROBLEMS WITH CONTRACTS:
(i) LACK OF CONSENSUS

Mathieson Gee (Ayrshire) Ltd v *Quigley* 1952 SC (HL) 38

Court: House of Lords (Scottish case)

Issue: *Consensus in idem* and the conclusion of contract in a situation in which the parties were not in dispute about whether there was a contract.

Facts: Dr Quigley owned a property in Renfrewshire and wanted to have mould removed from a large pond on his property. He received a letter from the company he had asked to quote for the work: "We refer to our visit on Monday last and confirm that we are prepared to supply the necessary mechanical plant for the excavation and removal …".

He replied: "I have to acknowledge with thanks the receipt of your letter of 2nd instant and have pleasure in confirming my verbal acceptance telephoned this afternoon of your offer to remove the silt and deposit from the pond at Bankhead House, near Rutherglen …".

Claim: The original claim was for payment. Dr Quigley had paid part of the bill and was being sued for the remainder. This dispute over payment went to the Outer House of the Court of Session and then to the Inner House. The Inner House increased the sum payable by Dr Quigley but Lord Carmont dissented, saying that there was no *consensus in idem* and so no contract at all. Dr Quigley took his case to the House of Lords, arguing that either the amount due by him to the contractors should be reduced to the amount agreed by the Outer House or, alternatively, there was no contract and so the action for payment should be dismissed.

Judgment: Lord Reid said that the court had to decide wether it was open to it to find that there was no contract and agreed that it was. If there was no contract, the court could not then be asked to make a judgment on its terms. The action was dismissed.

Lord Reid quoted another case with approval at p 43 of the judgment: "If authority be necessary for this I find it in the speech of Lord Loreburn, L.C., in *Houldsworth* v. *Gordon Cumming*, where he said: 'It is not enough for the parties to agree in saying there was a concluded contract if there was none, and then to ask a judicial decision as to what the contract in fact was. That would be the same thing as asking us to make the bargain, whereas our sole function is to interpret it.'"

Analysis: The court is entitled to determine whether a contract exists at all before determining claims under it. In this case, the parties were clearly at cross purposes, with the contractors offering to supply appropriate equipment only and Dr Quigley "accepting" on the basis that they would do the work.

PROBLEMS WITH CONTRACTS:
(ii) LACK OF CONSENT

Stobo Ltd v *Morrisons (Gowns) Ltd* 1949 SC 184

Court: Inner House, Court of Session

Issue: Whether a contract existed when the "agreement" was made "subject to contract".

Facts: The pursuers (tobacconists) and the defenders (clothes retailers) were tenants of neighbouring shops. The landlords decided to sell the shops and the defenders bought both of them. Before the sale went through, the pursuers and defenders had agreed that the defenders would then sell one of the shops to the pursuers "subject to contract". After the sale by the landlords was settled, the defenders decided not to sell on one of the shops to the pursuers.

Claim: The pursuers brought an action for specific implement (ie an action asking the court to grant an order to make the defenders fulfil the "contract"). The pursuers claimed that there was a contract for the sale but the defenders argued that there was no contract.

Decision: In this case there was no contract to be enforced and so the action failed. Important note: this decision was based on the full facts which included important facts about the timing of letters etc and not on the mere inclusion of the words "subject to contract".

Judgment: The Lord President (Lord Cooper) said at p 197: "The only rules of Scots law which it appears to me to be possible to extract from past decisions and general principles are that it is perfectly possible for the parties to an apparent contract to provide that there shall be *locus poenitentiae* until the terms of their agreement have been reduced to a formal contract; but that the bare fact that the parties to a completed agreement stipulated that it shall be embodied in a formal contract does not necessarily import that they are still in the stage of negotiation. In each instance it is a matter of the construction of the correspondence in the light of the facts, proved or averred, on which side of the border-line the case lies. I refer in support of these rules to the weighty pronouncements of Lord Wensleydale in *Chinnock* v. *Marchioness of Ely* (1865) 4 De G., J. & Sm. 638, of Lord Chancellor Cairns in *Rossiter* v. *Miller*, 3 App. Cas. 1124 at pp. 1137 ff., and of Lord Chancellor Finlay in *Gordon's Exrs.*, 1918, 1 S.L.T. 407."

Analysis: The law will determine the point at which the contract is concluded and will not rely on mere words or labels. The words "subject to contract" do not operate to prevent conclusion of contract in and of themselves.

Small v Fleming 2003 SCLR 647

Court: Outer House, Court of Session

Issue: Was there a contract of joint venture or not when heads of agreement had been drafted but not signed?

Facts: The two parties were interested in setting up a joint venture to buy land. They discussed finance and Small drafted the heads of agreement for the terms of the offer they were going to make on the land. However, Fleming took professional advice and decided not to proceed with the joint venture. Instead, he went on alone with an offer on the land.

Claim: Small claimed that there was a contract for the joint venture which Fleming had breached. Fleming denied that there had been sufficient agreement to conclude the contract.

Decision: No contract. The heads of agreement were merely indicative of the sorts of things that should be considered if the parties went ahead. Many of the key points in the formation and operation of the joint venture had not been agreed: no consensus.

Judgment: The Lord Ordinary was referred to Viscount Dunedin's statement in *May & Butcher Ltd* v *The King* [1934] 2 KB 17 at 21:

"To be a good contract there must be a concluded bargain, and a concluded contract is one which settles everything that is necessary to be settled and leaves nothing to be settled by agreement between the parties. Of course it may leave something which still has to be determined, but then that determination must be a determination which does not depend upon the agreement between the parties. In the system of law in which I was brought up, that was expressed by one of those brocards of which perhaps we have been too fond, but which often express very neatly what is wanted: '*Certum est quod certum reddi potest*'. ... What are the essentials may vary according to the particular contract under consideration."

and decided that there was insufficient agreement in this case on the facts.

Analysis: Heads of agreement are a useful tool in business as parties negotiate deals. However, they may or may not constitute a binding contract in their own right – each case has to be looked at on its own merits to find out how much consensus is actually there and if the balance is against consensus then no contract will be found.

Walker v *Milne* (1823) 2 S 379

Court: Inner House, Court of Session

Issue: Recovery of pre-contractual expenses (also known as "Melville Monument liability").

Facts: Walker owned land in Edinburgh and was developing it with his father to create part of the New Town. Subscribers wanted to erect a statue of Viscount Melville on this land and, with Walker's permission, entered the Coates Estate and made some preparations including digging up land and interrupting development of the area. The subscribers then decided to locate their statue elsewhere and took it to St Andrew Square, Edinburgh.

Claim: Walker sued for breach of contract and repayment of expenditure.

Decision: There was no written contract as required for heritage but Walker was entitled to payment for costs incurred.

Judgment: It seems that there was an agreement here, albeit one that was not reduced to writing as required by law, and that was decisive in allowing reimbursement of costs.

Analysis: This is the famous "Melville Monument" case in which it was held that one party may be reimbursed by the other for a "breach" of pre-contract. However, in this case, there does appear to have been an agreement between the parties but it was not reduced to writing and so not a binding contract at that time. Treat with caution following *Dawson International plc* v *Coats Paton plc* 1988 SLT 854 and *Khaliq* v *Londis (Holdings) Ltd* [2010] CSIH 13 (both below).

Dawson International plc v Coats Paton plc 1988 SLT 854

Court: Inner House, Court of Session

Issue: Whether costs of a failed merger could be recovered from the other party in the absence of a contract.

Facts: Dawson International plc and Coats Paton plc were in discussions about merging. This would involve Dawson buying Coats' shares. The parties agreed that this should be an agreed merger, ie no other competing bids were to be sought. They got as far as issuing a joint press statement setting out the planned merger and the terms of the offer for the shares. The pursuers organised printing of the offer documents to be issued on 10 February 1986. (Note: in a case involving two publicly quoted companies, such transactions involve huge amounts of paperwork to comply with Companies Acts, Stock Exchange Rules etc and costly financial and legal advice.) However, a second buyer had come onto the scene in the meantime and despite two of the directors of Coats telling Dawson that the second buyer would not be encouraged, it was announced on 10 February 1986 that the second buyer was indeed to take it over (ie buy its shares). Dawson's bid was therefore dead in the water and all the legal, accounting and printing work carried out in connection with this bid had been in vain.

Claim: Dawson sued on two grounds: (1) it sued Coats for damages for breach of contract and, alternatively, if no contract found (2) it sued for reimbursement of costs arising out of misrepresentation by the company and the two directors. The first ground went to the Inner House to decide in 1993. Much of this case centres on interpretation of company law and duties of directors etc but there is important discussion of the "Melville Monument liability".

Decision: The Inner House held that the expenditure was not repayable.

Judgment: In the first action, the court discussed the so-called "Melville Monument liability" for breach in pre-contractual cases. Lord Cullen at p 866A analysed the issue in these terms:

> "I come now to the main issue which divided the parties. Having reviewed the cases in this field to which I was referred I am not satisfied that they provide authority for reimbursement of expenditure by one party occasioned by the representations of another beyond the case where the former acted in reliance on the implied assurance by the latter that there was a binding contract between them when in fact there was no more than an agreement which fell short of being a binding contract. … It is significant that *Walker* v *Milne* has never been explicitly recognised as an authority for reimbursement in a case in which parties had not reached an agreement. … It is clear that the law does not favour the recovery of expenditure made merely in the hope or expectation of agreement being entered into or of a stated intention being fulfilled. See *Gilchrist* v *Whyte*, per Lord Ardwall at 1907 S.C., at p.994, and *Gray* v *Johnston*, per Lord Hunter at 1928 S.L.T. [499 at] p.506 and Lord Justice Clerk Alness at p.510."

Analysis: "Melville Monument liability" for pre-contractual expenses is very limited in scope and the summary of the law by Lord Cullen suggests an even more narrow interpretation. It will apply only if one party incurs costs on the assurance of the other party that there is a binding agreement, when in fact there is not. The later case of *Khaliq* v *Londis (Holdings) Ltd* [2010] CSIH 13 pours more cold water on the notion that such costs can be recovered.

Aisling Developments Ltd v *Persimmon Homes plc* [2008] CSOH 140

Court: Outer House, Court of Session

Issue: Whether a contract requiring formal writing but lacking same had been "cured" by s 1(3) and (4) of the Requirements of Writing (Scotland) Act 1995.

Facts: Aisling was a company which provided services connected with the development of land (eg handling planning applications, reports etc to developers). Queen Margaret University College

("QMUC") was looking for a new site and Aisling knew that Persimmon owned land in the area QMUC wanted and that, although, on the face of it, it was green belt land which would not attract planning permission for development, building by an educational establishment might be much more likely. Rather than simply introduce QMUC to Persimmon, Aisling wanted to capitalise on this knowledge itself. It entered into an exclusivity agreement with Persimmon whereby it would negotiate exclusively to buy 70 acres of Persimmon land and sell 25 acres of other land to Persimmon for housing (these 25 acres would come from the QMUC existing site). Aisling would secure those 25 acres from QMUC by giving it 35 acres of the Persimmon land once acquired. On 5 March 2002, there was a meeting between all three parties at which the transaction was discussed in detail. However, written missives for the transfer of land were never concluded: on 25 August 2006, Persimmon advised Aisling that it was "withdrawing from negotiations".

Claim: Aisling as pursuers claimed that notwithstanding the lack of formal writing, there was a contract for the sale and purchase of land under s 1(3) and (4) of the Requirements of Writing (Scotland) Act 1995 (ie the statutory rules which cure defects in lack of formal writing). The defenders denied that there was a contract at all: key elements had not been agreed upon.

Decision: There was no contract, even applying the rules in s 1(3) and (4) of the 1995 Act, because there was no evidence of "acquiescence" as required by the Act on Persimmon's part.

Judgment: The application of the "cure" fell foul of the facts here. There was no discussion of other remedies for "breach of pre-contractual remedies". The judge repeated the general rule that, in commercial cases, the courts will generally prefer to find that there is a contract than that there is not. The judgment of Lord President Clyde in *R & J Dempster* v *Motherwell Bridge and Engineering Co* 1964 SC 308 at pp 327–328 was quoted with approval:

> "when a court of law is asked to construe a commercial arrangement couched in terms which are *prima facie* obligatory, and which are acted on by the parties as obligatory, the court will prefer a construction which gives the contract binding effect. For the essence of commerce is making bargains, and unenforceable arrangements are the exception and not the rule."

Analysis: A useful case on the statutory rules in the Requirements of Writing (Scotland) Act 1995 which replaced the common law rules of *rei interventus* and homologation. These rules can cure a lack of formal writing if the tests in them are met.

Khaliq v *Londis (Holdings) Ltd* [2010] CSIH 13

Court: Inner House, Court of Session

Issue: Whether a businessman could claim back monies spent fitting out shops in anticipation of getting membership of a trading group.

Facts: Mr Khaliq owned two shop units and ran a fast food shop from one of them. He wanted to join a trading group called Londis and develop another business: Londis provided wholesale goods to its members and other services. He had discussions with Londis and its representative told him that he should use the superior of his two shops as his "Londis" shop and to use a Londis-approved shop fitter to carry out the work if he wanted to be part of the group. This necessitated Mr Khaliq's moving his fast food business to the other unit. He signed an application form and paid the joining fee of £50. In April 2003, the Londis representative showed him an e-mail which appeared to say that his membership was approved and they worked together on his Londis project over the next few months. In February 2004, Mr Khaliq received an e-mail to say that his membership application was not going through. Mr Khaliq had already spent a lot of money doing up his shops and transferring the fast food business.

Claim: An earlier claim for breach of contract was rejected at sheriff court level as there was no contract to enforce. This claim was for "Melville Monument liability" instead – breach of pre-contractual negotiations, founded upon an "unenforceable agreement". The respondents, Londis, argued that the "Melville Monument liability" was no longer good law since (1) the passing of the Civil Evidence (Scotland) Act 1988 which abolishes the need for corroboration in Scots civil law; (2) the Requirements of Writing (Scotland) Act 1995 which sets out the statutory rules on what used to be covered by the common law rules of *rei interventus* and homologation and is "more generous" than the previous common law; and (3) the growth of delictual liability for negligent misrepresentation, meaning there was no longer a need for this type of liability to plug the gaps.

Decision: No liability attached to Londis.

Judgment: The grounds for "Melville Monument liability" were not found to be in place here (that test includes that it should be "unconscionable" that the remedy is not granted) so the court did not have to decide whether the law was still sound. However, Lord Osborne considered it at p 26:

> "In relation to this formulation of the law, arrived at in 1988, it appears to me that certain subsequent developments may have gone a long way to removing the equitable justification which, in earlier times, was seen as underlying the Melville Monument principle. I have in mind, the provisions of section 1 of the Civil Evidence (Scotland) Act 1988, which abolished the rule requiring corroboration in civil proceedings, sections 1 and 2 of Requirements of Writing (Scotland) Act 1995, which relaxed the requirements of the law in relation to certain kinds of contract relating to heritable property, and the developments that have occurred in the law relating particularly to negligent misrepresentation. Thus, in an appropriate case, there may be justification for reconsideration of the raison d'être, or at least the scope, of Melville Monument liability. However, in the particular circumstances of this case, I do not find it necessary to undertake such reconsideration."

Analysis: The *obiter dictum* in this case is the most interesting part. It casts doubt on whether "Melville Monument liability" is still good law. We need a case in point where that law is directly at issue for that judicial debate to move forward. Meanwhile, treat this case with caution.

Balfour v *Balfour* [1919] 2 KB 571

Court: Court of Appeal (English case)

Issue: Enforceability of a domestic arrangement.

Facts: A couple made a verbal agreement that the husband would send the wife £30 per month while she was in England recovering from illness and he was back home in Sri Lanka (then Ceylon) where they lived. Later, they broke up and Mrs Balfour wanted her husband to continue making the payments but he did not.

Claim: Mrs Balfour claimed breach of contract.

Decision: There was no breach of contract because this was a straightforward domestic agreement and not enforceable as a matter of contract.

Judgment: Duke LJ at p 573: "In order to establish a contract there ought to be something more than mere mutual promises having regard to the domestic relations of the parties. It is required that the obligations arising out of that relationship shall be displaced before either of the parties can found a contract upon such promises."

Analysis: *Normal* domestic arrangements do not give rise to contractual obligations

Robertson v *Anderson* 2003 SLT 235

Court: Inner House, Court of Session

Issue: Would the court recognise and enforce a contract between friends to split bingo winnings?

Facts: Mrs Robertson and Mrs Anderson were friends who had a long-standing agreement to share bingo winnings equally if one of them was lucky enough to win. Mrs Anderson won £108,000 but refused to share it as agreed.

Claim: Mrs Robertson claimed £54,000 (half of Mrs Anderson's winnings). The Outer House awarded it but the defender then reclaimed to the Inner House, arguing that the Lord Ordinary had not been entitled to make that decision and that since the agreement was made in a social context it was not legally binding. Even if it was legally binding, it was a gaming contract (*sponsione ludicra*) and not enforceable at that time. This event pre-dates the coming into force of s 335 of the Gambling Act 2005 which allows gaming or gambling contracts to be enforced. Previously, the common law did not allow such contracts to be enforced.

Decision: The Inner House agreed with the Lord Ordinary – this was legally enforceable because the facts pointed to serious intentions and this being a commercial matter, albeit one discussed in a social context. Furthermore, it was not of itself a *sponsione ludicra*.

Judgment: "Although no Scottish authority was cited to us on this aspect of the case, we note that the issue of contractual intention was considered in the case of *Dawson International Plc* v *Coats Paton Plc*. In his opinion in that case, Lord Prosser observed (at 1993 SLT, p 95): 'Speaking generally, I would accept that when two parties are talking to one another about a matter which has commercial significance to both, a statement by one party that he will do some particular thing will normally be construed as obligatory, or as an offer, rather than a mere statement of intention, if the words and deeds of the other party indicate that the statement was so understood, and the obligation confirmed or the offer accepted so that parties appeared to regard the commercial "deal" as concluded. But in considering whether there is indeed a contract between the parties, in any particular case, it will always be essential to look at the particular facts, with a view to discovering whether these facts, rather than some general rule of thumb, can be said to reveal consensus and an intention to conclude a contract'. Whether the context is social or commercial, however – and, these not being watertight compartments, some cases will concern contexts which contain elements of both – it is, as Lord Prosser said, essential to look at the particular facts to discover whether those facts reveal an intention to conclude a contract."

Analysis: The apparently social context of an agreement will not necessarily determine whether there is intention to be legally binding or not – the court will look at all of the facts to determine whether intention is there.

PROBLEMS WITH CONTRACTS:
(iii) LACK OF CAPACITY

Taylor v *Provan* (1864) 2 M 1226

Court: Inner House, Court of Session

Issue: Is contractual capacity compromised by intoxication?

Facts: Provan offered to buy cows from Taylor but would not pay the price asked. However, he changed his mind after drinking alcohol but, on sobering up, regretted his decision.

Claim: Taylor wanted to enforce the contract but Provan asked the court to reduce it.

Decision: The court upheld the contract.

Judgment: The degree of intoxication can vary and in order to result in lack of capacity, it must be of sufficient degree to render the person incapacitated.

Analysis: Intoxication can affect capacity but it must be sufficiently serious to have that effect.

Pollok v Burns (1875) 2 R 497

Court: Inner House, Court of Session

Issue: Capacity and intoxication.

Facts: Sir Hew Pollok signed a bill of exchange (a form of negotiable instrument) when very drunk and 6 months later sought to have it suspended.

Claim: Sir Hew claimed that he had been *incapax* when the bill was signed and so should not be bound by it.

Decision: The court decided that the bill should not be suspended.

Judgment: Lord Justice-Clerk Moncrieff held that if someone is in this position, he should take steps immediately on sobering up to challenge his actions. Sir Hew had taken far too long, which suggested to his Lordship that he had in fact had capacity and that he "knew what he was doing".

Analysis: Intoxication can lead to loss of capacity but remedial steps must be taken right away if this is to form the basis of a challenge, suggesting that this is not sufficient to render the contract void but rather voidable (challengeable).

Cantiere San Rocco v Clyde Shipbuilding Co 1923 SC (HL) 105

Court: House of Lords (Scottish case)

Issue: Frustration of contract when a party to a contract becomes an enemy alien and subsequent grounds for claiming repayment of monies paid on conclusion of contract for goods which were never received.

Facts: Cantiere, an Austrian company, ordered engines from Clyde, a Scottish company, and paid the first instalment of the price on signature of the contract. However, the First World War broke out before any parts were made. By law, the contract could not be performed after war was declared but Clyde did not want to repay the instalment.

Claim: After the war, Cantiere sued for repayment of the instalment paid.

Decision: The contract had been frustrated (ie could not be performed through no fault of either party) but the defenders had to repay the money (less any reasonable costs incurred). In other words, Clyde had to make restitution; the Roman remedy of *condictio causa data causa non secuta* applied.

Judgment: There is an excellent discussion of the Roman law principles and adoption into Scots law (ie *restitutio* and the *condictio*) in the judgments, for example the Earl of Birkenhead's judgment at paras 109 *et seq*:

> "First, as to the Roman law. This is treated in the Digest and other authoritative texts in connexion with the procedure known as *Condictio*. This process was available to recover money or things which had been parted with by the owner, at such a time as he became entitled to reclaim them. The *Condictio* was only a single form of action, but it was grouped or classified in various ways, according to the kind of property or according to the *causa* which gave occasion for recourse to the *Condictio*; … The underlying principle of the *Condictio* was that a person had received from another some property, and that, by reason of circumstances existing at the time or arising afterwards, it was or became contrary to honesty and fair dealing for the recipient to retain it. The particular case which is in point is the *Condictio causa data causa non secuta*. … The rule may, I think, be fairly stated thus: A person who had given to another any money or other property for a purpose which had failed could recover what he had given, except where there had been no fault on the recipient's part, and he had not been enriched thereby. If the recipient had been enriched, then he would, if the purpose failed and he retained the property, be acting unjustly, and, consequently, he was under an obligation to return it. It was open to him to show, not merely that he had not been enriched at all, but also, if such were the fact, that though enriched he had not benefited to the full value of the property. Such would be the case if the property had been lost or damaged without blame attaching to him. Such being the Roman law as embodied in the *Corpus Juris Civilis*, it now becomes necessary to examine the application of the rule in Scotland."

His Lordship went on to consider passages from Stair's *Institutions*, Book I, Title VII, para 7; Bankton (Book I, Title VIII, para 23); Bell's *Principles* (section 530); Erskine; and Lord Inglis's judgment in *Watson* v *Shankland*:

"… On principle I cannot see any reason for holding that the outbreak of war leads to any result different from that which follows, as I have shown, from any other act or event beyond the control of the parties. There has been a payment on account of the supplying of the complete set of engines, not a payment of any particular part or stage, so that there was no allocation to any specific thing to be done or made. The set of engines has not been supplied, and for the failure to supply no one is to blame. There has been in fact a *causa non secuta*."

Analysis: Frustration of contract by war could lead to restitution on the ground of unjust enrichment in Scots law. English law would have reached a different conclusion.

PROBLEMS WITH CONTRACTS:
(iv) LACK OF FORMALITY

Advice Centre for Mortgages v *McNicoll* [2006] CSOH 58

Court: Outer House, Court of Session

Issue: Whether real rights had been created in a lease, using the Requirements of Writing (Scotland) Act 1995 to cure a lack of formal writing.

Facts: Advice Centre were in negotiations with the owner of the property in question to take a lease of it for 10 years, with an option to buy at some point. They had received an offer of lease in 1999 from the owner's agents and replied through their agents in May 2000. these letters were referred to as the "missives". However, missives were not concluded: there was an offer, a qualified acceptance (or counter-offer) but no concluding letter. There was an unsigned lease and draft offer dating from October 2000 which the parties referred to as the "lease". Nevertheless, they moved in. Frances McNicoll later bought the property. In order for a successor landlord to be bound by a lease or option to buy, the tenant must have acquired a real right and not just a personal right. A personal right was enforceable only against the original landlords. Ms McNicoll wanted the Advice Centre to move out.

Claim: Advice Centre raised an action for declarator that they were in fact tenants of the property either on the basis of the "missives" or on the basis of the "lease", with real rights and had the right to exercise an option to buy the property in the "lease". The new owner, Ms McNicoll, disputed this.

Decision: The missives were not concluded and there was no *consensus in idem*. The lease was not signed and so it was not in writing for the purpose of either the Requirements of Writing (Scotland) Act 1995 or the Leases Act 1449, compliance with which creates real rights in short leases (those under 20 years). The sections in the 1995 Act which can be used to cure defects in formal writing (s 1(3) and (4)) apply to personal rights and not to real rights and so could not be used to establish a real right under the lease. Thus the tenants had only personal rights, not real rights, and the lease with its option was not binding on the successor owner, Ms McNicoll (even although she had known all about this as she had been an employee of the former owners and knew about the "option").

Judgment: Lord Drummond Young gave this analysis of the relevant provisions of the 1995 Act at paras [16] *et seq*:

> "… it is obvious that they deal with the formal requirements of certain categories of legal act, including contracts relating to land. They are not concerned with the substance of the legal act concerned. Secondly, the formal requirements for contracts and other deeds falling within the specified categories are extremely simple and rational. It is not difficult to satisfy those requirements. In those circumstances, I am of opinion that there is no need to give the personal bar provisions in subss (3) and (4) of s 1 a liberal interpretation."

Analysis: The creation of real rights requires certain steps. Failure to take those steps will result in the lesser personal rights being created, which are not enforceable against the world: personal rights are only enforceable between the two parties to the original contract in the vast majority of cases. The statutory form of personal bar set out in s 1(3) and (4) of the Requirements of Writing (Scotland) Act 1995 cannot be used to cure defects in the execution of leases etc to create real rights: they can only be used to cure defects relating to contracts and other personal rights.

PROBLEMS WITH CONTRACTS:
(v) ILLEGALITY

Barr v *Crawford* 1983 SLT 481

Court: Outer House, Court of Session

Issue: Could a "contract of bribe" be enforced?

Facts: Mrs Barr claimed that she had paid over £8,000 to the then Provost of Falkirk and another member of the Licensing Board to secure the renewal of her husband's liquor licence and she wanted the money back when this failed to materialise. Criminal charges were brought for fraud and dealt with separately.

Claim: Mrs Barr launched a civil action to recover the money paid.

Decision: The civil claim could not succeed because the "contract" on which the claim was based was a *pactum illicitum* – an illegal contract.

Judgment: Lord Mayfield at p 483: "There was in my view illegality because the payment made by Mrs Barr was a bribe made in the course of a dishonest intention thus tainting the transaction. It can also be described more simply, perhaps, as a corrupt agreement. In my view, the averments of the pursuer indicate a corrupt intention that prevents the court from taking cognisance of the ground of action. I have reached the above conclusion on the facts and having been referred to Bell's *Principles*, s. 35, and *Gloag on Contract* in the chapter *'Pacta Illicita'* beginning at p 549."

Analysis: The courts will not enforce contracts which are illegal.

Pearce v *Brooks* (1866) LR 1 Ex 213

Court: English Court of Exchequer

Issue: Illegality in contract where use of subject-matter is for an illegal purpose.

Facts: The purchaser of a carriage on hire purchase was a prostitute and the carriage was for use in her (illegal) business. This fact was known to the hirers. The lady failed to keep up payments.

Claim: The hirers claimed for breach of contract.

Decision: The contract was unenforceable on the ground of public policy.

Judgment: The court held that the fact that the hirers knew the illegal purpose for which the hire contract had been entered into rendered it void and unenforceable.

Analysis: If the subject-matter of a contract is to be used in an illegal activity and this is known to the other party then this will render the contract unenforceable on the ground of illegality. Remember that the hirers were not engaged in prostitution themselves.

Dowling & Rutter v *Abacus Frozen Foods Ltd (No 2)* 2002 SLT 491

Court: Outer House, Court of Session

Issue: Did the illegal *performance* of a contract render it unenforceable?

Facts: The pursuers as employment agents supplied workers to the defenders but not all of the people supplied had the correct work permits, which meant that they were working illegally and the immigration authorities put a stop to it under the Asylum and Immigration Act 1996. The defenders refused to pay the bill for the work that had been done.

Claim: The pursuers were claiming for payment under the contract and the defenders refused on the ground that the contract was not enforceable, claiming that a contract *performed* illegally should be treated the same as one *formed* illegally. They also counter-claimed for financial loss suffered as a result of the workers being withdrawn and the pursuers failing to supply any more.

Decision: The contract was enforceable in this case but each case had to be judged on its merits and there was no single broad test

Judgment: Lord Johnston heard the proof (the civil equivalent of a trial, when facts are considered) and approved the reasoning of Lord Wheatley who heard an earlier debate in the case. Lord Wheatley at pp 493 *et seq* said:

"I have concluded that although there appears to be no comprehensive binding authority in Scotland on this subject, what authority there is tends to favour the idea that a different approach should be taken to contracts which are illegal in their formation, and contracts which are legal in construction but which are performed illegally. I think that the statement that the two kinds of contract illegality should be considered on exactly the same basis is too broad ... It must therefore follow that in such cases the court has to assess the nature and quality of the illegality before deciding whether any remedy is available; 'Illegality in contract admits of degree' (Gloag (2nd edn), p 549). The illegality may be statutory or at common law; and the illegality may be in the formation of the contract or in its implementation. If the illegality is statutory, the first question is whether it renders the contract void or illegal. If it renders the contract void, the court will have an opportunity to recognise the ancillary rights which arise out of the arrangements between the parties (as in *Cuthbertson* v *Lowes*). If the contract is illegal in its formation because of a statutory prohibition and the court will not enforce the contract for that reason, it will also presumably find it difficult if not impossible to enforce any rights which might arise incidentally out of the contract. This is because of the need to sustain the supremacy of statute law, and it also reflects the maxim *ex turpi causa non oritur actio*. The court will accordingly refuse such claims irrespective of the consequences."

At p 495G: "I do not think therefore that contracts which are affected by statutory illegality can admit of a universal treatment. In the case of a statutory illegality in the implementation of a contract, I consider that it is open to assess the degree of illegality involved and what effect that illegality should have on the contract, and on the rights of the parties arising therefrom."

Analysis: A contract which is performed illegally may be void or otherwise unenforceable but the court will look at whether it is a breach of common law or statute and at the degree and effect of illegality on the party's rights before deciding whether to allow it to stand or fall.

Bridge v *Deacons (A Firm)* [1984] AC 705

Court: Privy Council (this case originates in Hong Kong, then a British colony)

Issue: Enforcement of a restrictive covenant in a contract of partnership.

Facts: Mr Bridge joined a large firm of solicitors in Hong Kong and was made a partner. The partnership agreement stated that if a partner left the firm he would not be allowed, for a period of 5 years, to work for anyone who was or had been a client of the firm in the preceding 3 years. Mr Bridge worked in the Intellectual Property Department and had no contact with 90 per cent of the firm's clients. He retired in 1982 and the firm asked the court for an injunction (the English equivalent of an interdict) to enforce the restrictive covenant.

Claim: Mr Bridge appealed against the injunction, claiming that the covenant was unreasonable and so unenforceable as an illegal contract.

Decision: The court held that this clause was reasonable, taking all of the circumstances into account.

Judgment: Lord Fraser of Tullybelton delivered the judgment and said:

> "It is well-established law that covenants in restraint of trade are unenforceable unless they can be shown to be reasonable in the interests of the parties and in the public interest. The classic statement of the law is in the well-known passage in the speech of Lord Macnaghten in *Nordenfelt* v. *Maxim Nordenfelt Guns and Ammunition Co. Ltd* [1894] A.C. 535, 565:
>
> 'The public have an interest in every person's carrying on his trade freely: so has the individual. All interference with individual liberty of action in trading, and all restraints of trade of themselves, if there is nothing more, are contrary to public policy, and therefore void. That is the general rule. But there are exceptions: restraints of trade and interference with individual liberty of action may be justified by the special circumstances of a particular case. It is a sufficient justification, and indeed it is the only justification, if the restriction is reasonable – reasonable, that is, in reference to the interests of the parties concerned and reasonable in reference to the interests of the public, so framed and so guarded as to afford adequate

protection to the party in whose favour it is imposed, while at the same time it is in no way injurious to the public.'"

 The court stressed that it must ascertain what the legitimate interests of the party seeking to enforce the covenant are and then decide whether the terms of the restrictive covenant are enough or too much to do that.

Analysis: Restrictive covenants are *prima facie* illegal, so the courts will not be overly keen to enforce them. However, if the legitimate business interests are established and the terms of the clause are sufficient to protect those then this will be one exception to the rule.

Bluebell Apparel Ltd v *Dickinson* 1978 SC 16

Court: Inner House, Court of Session

Issue: Enforceability of restrictive covenants (1) prohibiting disclosure of trade secrets and (2) prohibiting ex-employees from working with competitors anywhere in the world for 2 years post employment.

Facts: Mr Dickinson worked for the company which manufactured Wrangler jeans and was privy to its trade secrets. After 6 months with the company, he decided to leave and join a rival company making Levi jeans.

Claim: Bluebell obtained an interim interdict (a temporary measure) against him to enforce both parts of the restrictive covenant. Full interdict was then granted in respect of the trade secrets part but the interim interdict was recalled in respect of the prohibition on working for competitors. Bluebell sought to have the interdict against that second part restored. Mr Dickinson argued that it was unreasonable, and so not enforceable, on three grounds: (1) it was worldwide; (2) it was too long at 2 years; and (3) it was too widely drawn (it prohibited any employment with competitors, not just in his current role).

Decision: Interim interdict restored for the prohibition on working for competitors. The court noted that a prohibition on disclosure of trade secrets by itself is fairly useless without an accompanying prohibition on working for competitors and held that the terms of this prohibition were reasonable in the circumstances, having regard to the legitimate interests to be protected.

Judgment: Lord President Emslie at p 29:

> "Is such a restriction too wide having regard to the legitimate
> interest of the petitioners to prevent their trade secrets from
> coming to the knowledge of any competitor of theirs? If it is
> accepted, as it must be at this stage, that the respondent is an
> employee in the possession of trade secrets which would be of
> value to any competitor of the petitioners in the world's jeans
> market and that the respondent has properly been interdicted
> *ad interim* from disclosing these secrets, the restriction, as we
> have construed it, is not *prima facie* unreasonable at all. The risk
> of trade secrets of the petitioners coming into the knowledge
> of rivals obviously arises whenever an employee in posses-
> sion of these secrets joins the ranks of a competitor for in the
> service of that competitor, in any capacity, anywhere in the
> world, the employee may deliberately or unwittingly enable
> the competitor to acquire the benefit of these trade secrets in
> the trade in which he is in competition with the petitioners."

Analysis: The court will examine the legitimate interests which the
party seeking to enforce the restrictive covenant is entitled to protect
and decide whether the covenant protects those interests or goes
beyond that. If it goes beyond, it will not be enforceable.

Stewart v Stewart (1899) 1 F 1158

Court: Inner House, Court of Session

Issue: Enforceability of restrictive covenant.

Facts: Mr Stewart was a photographer whose contract stated that he
could not work within a 20-mile radius of Elgin if he left his current
position. He left and duly commenced trading in the area.

Claim: Mr Stewart claimed that the restrictive covenant was not
enforceable.

Decision: The court disagreed and upheld it.

Judgment: The restrictive covenant could be enforced because it
was based on a reasonable geographical restriction, appropriate to
the rural area in question.

Analysis: Restrictive covenants can be enforced if reasonable and
the decision has to be made on a case-by-case basis.

Dallas McMillan & Sinclair v *Simpson* 1989 SLT 454

Court: Outer House, Court of Session

Issue: Mr Simpson was a partner in a firm of solicitors. The partnership agreement contained a restrictive covenant prohibiting any outgoing partner from working within a 20-mile radius of Glasgow Cross. Was it enforceable?

Facts: The partnership agreement stated: "Any of the parties hereto on ceasing to be a partner in terms of these presents shall not either directly or indirectly by himself or others representing him for the space of five years from and after ceasing to be a partner commence or carry on or assist in carrying on the business of a solicitor either alone or in connection with any other person or persons or as an employee except with the firm and that all within a radius of twenty miles from Glasgow Cross, it being agreed by all parties hereto that this time and distance are reasonable for the protection of the parties hereto and any in terms of these presents." Mr Simpson decided to leave to work for a rival firm. He also wanted to send out a letter to his clients, advising them that he was going and inviting them to join him.

Claim: The firm sought interim interdict to enforce the restrictive covenant and to prevent Mr Simpson from sending that letter. He argued that interdict should not be granted because the covenant was too widely drawn.

Decision: Lord Mayfield refused to grant interim interdict to enforce the restrictive covenant.

Judgment: Lord Mayfield said at p 457: "in my view the range of protection is far beyond what is necessary for the protection of the petitioners' legitimate interests … It may be that transfer of the respondent to another firm would result in some loss of existing clients but in my view clients cannot be stopped going elsewhere. It is understandable that the petitioners do not wish clients to follow the respondent. It is in my view, however, unreasonable to achieve that object by a covenant of such width and scope as [this]."

Analysis: A restrictive covenant which goes beyond protecting the legitimate interests of the party seeking to rely on it will not be enforced.

Mulvein v *Murray* 1908 SC 528

Court: Inner House, Court of Session

Issue: Could different parts of a restrictive covenant be enforced separately if part was legal and part illegal?

Facts: Mr Murray was a salesman for Mr Mulvein and his contract stated that if his position was terminated "the said John Murray binds himself not to sell to or to canvass any of the said George Mulvein's customers, or to sell or travel in any of the towns or districts traded in by the said George Mulvein for a period of twelve months from the date of the termination of this engagement". Mr Murray left.

Claim: Mr Mulvein obtained an interdict prohibiting Mr Murray from selling or travelling in named areas where the pursuer had traded. Mr Murray appealed against it.

Decision: The restrictive covenant had two parts. The part prohibiting Mr Murray from canvassing customers for 12 months was severable and could be validly enforced (although actually the 12 months had expired so no interdict granted) but the second part ("to sell or travel in any of the towns or districts") was too wide and not severable in that it could not be redrafted by the court to link it to the pursuer's designation as the seller, thus limiting it.

Judgment: Lord Ardwall said at p 535: "I regard the obligation as one and indivisible, and not separable or restrictable in part as suggested by the pursuer."

Analysis: If the court thinks that a covenant is not severable, it will not enforce the parts that would be reasonable if severable. The court will not redraft the covenant either.

Nordenfelt v *Maxim Nordenfelt Guns and Ammunition Co Ltd* [1894] AC 535

Court: House of Lords (English case)

Issue: Enforceability of a world-wide restrictive covenant of 25 years' duration.

Facts: Mr Nordenfelt sold his patents and business to a new company and contracted as follows:

'The said Thorsten Nordenfelt shall not, during the term of twenty-five years from the date of the incorporation of the company if the company shall so long continue to carry on business, engage except on behalf of the company either directly or indirectly in the trade or business of a manufacturer of guns, gun mountings or carriages, gunpowder, explosives or ammunition, or in any business competing or liable to compete in any way with that for the time being carried on by the company, provided that such restriction shall not apply to explosives other than gunpowder or to subaqueous or submarine boats or torpedoes or castings or forgings of steel or iron or alloys of iron or of copper. Provided also that the said Thorsten Nordenfelt shall not be released from this restriction by the company ceasing to carry on business merely for the purposes of re-constitution or with a view to the transfer of the business thereof to another company so long as such other company taking a transfer thereof shall continue to carry on the same."

He then entered into contracts with other gun and ammunition businesses.

Claim: The company sought to enforce the restraint in trade through an injunction (the English version of interdict). The Court of Appeal found the clause valid as "it relates to the trade or business of a manufacturer of guns, gun mountings or carriages, gunpowder, explosives or ammunition (except explosives other than gunpowder or subaqueous or submarine boats or torpedoes or castings or forgings of steel or iron or alloys of iron or of copper" (at p 536). Mr Nordenfelt appealed.

Decision: The restraint of trade was valid even although it was a general one, unlimited in space.

Judgment: Lord Herschell LC discussed the traditional distinction between partial and general restraints of trade, the latter being generally invalid, but decided (at pp 548 *et seq*) that a blanket ban on general covenants was too simplistic:

"I think that a covenant entered into in connection with the sale of the goodwill of a business must be valid where the full benefit of the purchase cannot be otherwise secured to the purchaser. It has been recognised in more than one case that it is to the advantage of the public that there should be free scope for the sale of the goodwill of a business or calling. These were cases of partial restraint. But it seems to me that if there be occupations where a sale of the goodwill would be greatly impeded, if not prevented, unless a general covenant could be obtained by the purchaser, there are no grounds of public policy which countervail the disadvantage which would arise if the goodwill were in such cases rendered unsaleable."

Analysis: There are exceptions to the general rule that restraints of trade are unenforceable and contrary to public policy. Those exceptions can evolve as commerce evolves. Even a very wide restraint of trade may be enforceable if it is required to protect the interests of the party seeking to enforce it. In this case, it protected the goodwill of a business with world-wide reach.

Dumbarton Steamboat Co Ltd v *MacFarlane* (1899) 1 F 993

Court: Inner House, Court of Session

Issue: A restraint of trade clause in a contract for the sale of business was challenged as being wider than reasonably necessary.

Facts: Mr MacFarlane sold his business to the Steamboat Company. A clause in the contract of sale stated that the vendor, Mr MacFarlane, should not "carry on or be concerned in a business of a like or similar kind in the United Kingdom for a period of ten years" from date of sale. It also stated that he would "do nothing to induce the … customers to cease dealing with the company". He stayed on as a manager of the business as an employee of the Steamboat Company but was dismissed. He started up his own rival business in Dumbarton soon afterwards and also began to solicit customers from the Steamboat Company which sought to interdict him from soliciting old customers but also to enforce the wider restraint of trade through an interdict.

Claim: The Steamboat Company argued that, in addition to enforcing a contractual prohibition against soliciting customers, it also had the right to enforce the wider restraint of trade clause as drafted because it had done some business nationally and was empowered to do so under its Articles of Association. It made an alternative argument (*esto*), that if it was indeed too wide in terms of the law, it should be enforced against Mr MacFarlane in and around Dumbarton. Mr MacFarlane argued that the clause was patently too wide and so the whole clause should be struck out and not enforced.

Judgment: Their Lordships agreed that it was quite right to interdict Mr MacFarlane from soliciting customers per the contract but that they could not enforce the wider restraint of trade which would have prevented Mr MacFarlane from carrying on his business anywhere in the UK. The Lord Justice-Clerk said at p 996: "the respondents have taken advantage of the appeal to make a further demand that the interdict be extended. For this I can see no reasonable ground. The whole business of the appellant was, and the whole business of the respondents is, carried on within a very limited area, and I think it would be quite unreasonable that by any interdict to be pronounced the power of the appellant to carry on business in other parts of the country should be excluded".

As for the alternative argument for restricting the ban to the Dumbarton area, Lord Trayner said at p 997: "The pursuers said that they would be satisfied if the defender was interdicted from carrying on the business of carrier between Glasgow and Dumbarton. But that was not contracted for. If the restraint, as the parties themselves expressed it, is not valid, then I think it must be disregarded. The Court cannot remake the contract for the parties."

Analysis: Restraint of trade clauses in sales of businesses will be enforced as drafted only if reasonable and one must look at the parameters within which the business was operated pre-sale to see what is reasonable. If not, the clause cannot be enforced: the court will not edit it to make it reasonable.

Esso Petroleum Co Ltd v *Harpers Garages (Stourport) Ltd*
[1976] QB 801

Court: Court of Appeal (English case)

Issue: Enforceability of restraint of trade clauses in a *solus* agreement.

Facts: Esso entered into agreements with Harpers to supply them with petrol for two tied garages. One of the garages was subject to a mortgage (standard security in Scots law) by Harpers in favour of Esso for a 21-year period and the sales agreement also ran for 21 years. The agreement restricted Harpers to operating within agreed rules, for example only selling petrol at Esso's retail prices and so on. Esso wrote to dealers, changing the terms of the agreements, and Harpers started selling rival brand petrol and advised that they wanted to redeem the mortgage.

Claim: Esso sought injunctions (the English equivalent of interdicts) to enforce the *solus* agreements and to prevent Harpers from selling rivals' petrol.

Decision: These agreements could be dealt with under the law of restraint of trade and so were subject to the rules about when they can be enforced as an exception to the general rule that they are void. The shorter *solus* agreement was enforceable as the 5-year period was appropriate to protect Esso's legitimate interests but the 21-year agreement was not enforceable as the length of time was longer than necessary to protect their interests.

Judgment: Lord Reid said at pp 298 *et seq*: "In my view this agreement is within the scope of the doctrine of restraint of trade as it had been developed in English law. Not only have the respondents agreed negatively not to sell other petrol but they have agreed positively to keep this garage open for the sale of the appellants' petrol at all reasonable hours throughout the period of the tie. It was argued that this was merely regulating the respondent's trading and rather promoting than restraining his trade. But regulating a person's existing trade may be a greater restraint than prohibiting him from engaging in a new trade and a contract to take one's whole supply from one source may be much more hampering than a contract to sell one's whole output to one buyer. I would not attempt to define the dividing line between contracts which are and contracts which are not in restraint of trade, but in my view this contract must be held to be in restraint of trade. So it is necessary to consider whether its provisions can be justified."

Analysis: A *solus* agreement in which one party is bound to supply only the goods of another is a restraint of trade and is subject to the usual rules on restraint of trade.

PROBLEMS WITH CONTRACTS:
(vi) RESTRICTIONS ON FREEDOM TO CONTRACT

W & S Pollock v *Macrae* 1922 SC (HL) 192

Court: House of Lords (Scottish case)

Issue: Enforceability of exclusion clause in contract for sale of engines.

Facts: Mr Macrae bought engines for his fishing boat from W & S Pollock. The contract for the sale stated: "2. Whilst we undertake to do our best to execute every order within the promised time, we do not accept responsibility for any direct or indirect losses which may arise if the completion is retarded by faulty castings or forging, strikes, lock-outs, non-delivery of material or parts by other manufacturers, or any other unforeseen circumstances, as no provision against the same is made in our price. ... 5. All goods are supplied on the condition that we shall not be liable for any direct or consequential damages arising from defective material or workmanship, even when such goods are supplied under the usual form of guarantee."

The engines were installed but almost immediately problems began.

Claim: W & S Pollock wanted final payment but Mr Macrae's claim was for damages for breach of contract because the engines did not work properly.

Decision: The House of Lords allowed Mr Macrae's claim.

Judgment: The exclusion clause as drafted did not cover the fundamental breach of contract in this case.

Analysis: Although the exclusion clause would appear to be fairly comprehensive in this case, it is a useful reminder that the court will interpret these clauses strictly. Here, Mr Macrae did not have working engines which was the purpose of the contract and the clause did not exclude liability to that extent.

McCrone v *Boots Farm Sales* 1981 SC 68, 1981 SLT 103

Court: Outer House, Court of Session

Issue: Were standard printed terms incorporated into a contact and, if so, did they amount to a "standard form contact" for the purposes of s 17 of the Unfair Contract Terms Act 1977?

Facts: Mr McCrone was a farmer who bought weed killer from Boots following a visit from their salesman. He had his potato crop sprayed with it but weeds grew and choked the crop, resulting in loss of value. He sued Boots for the loss, based on a breach of the Sale of Goods Act 1893.

Claim: Mr McCrone sued Boots, claiming that the weed killer was not fit for purpose under the Sale of Goods Act 1893 (this sale took place before the 1979 Act). They defended the action on the basis that there was an exclusion clause in their terms and conditions to the effect that s 14(3) of the 1893 Act did not apply. They also said that the contract was not a standard form contract and so the exclusion clause was valid but hedged their bets by using an *esto* (alternative) argument that if it was deemed by the court to be a standard form contract, the exclusion of liability was still permissible as it was fair and reasonable.

Decision: The court allowed the defenders the opportunity to amend their pleadings (written arguments in civil cases) to give more detail on why their terms should be deemed to be incorporated into the contract. The court held that the contract was standard form.

Judgment: Lord Dunpark said at p 74 on the meaning of "standard form contract":

> "Since Parliament saw fit to leave the phrase to speak for itself, far be it from me to attempt to formulate a comprehensive definition of it. However, the terms of section 17 in the context of this Act make it plain to me that the section is designed to prevent one party to a contract from having his contractual rights, against a party who is in breach of contract, excluded or restricted by a term or condition, which is one of a number of fixed terms or conditions invariably incorporated in contracts of the kind in question by the party in breach, and which have been incorporated in the particular contract in circumstances in which it would be unfair and unreasonable for the other party to have his rights so excluded or restricted. If the section

is to achieve its purpose, the phrase 'standard form contract' cannot be confined to written contracts in which both parties use standard forms. It is, in my opinion, wide enough to include any contract, whether wholly written or partly oral, which includes a set of fixed terms or conditions which the proponer applies, without material variation, to contracts of the kind in question. It would, therefore, include this contract if the defenders' General Conditions of Sale are proved to have been incorporated in it. In that event, it would be for the defenders to prove that it was fair and reasonable for their Condition 6 to be incorporated in this contract."

Analysis: A "standard form contract" for the purposes of the Sale of Goods Act includes any contract with a set of fixed terms which the party putting forward applies without much variation to all contracts of that type.

Director General of Fair Trading v *First National Bank*
[2002] 1 All ER 97

Court: House of Lords (English case)

Issue: Interpretation of the term "adequacy" in the Unfair Terms in Consumer Contracts Regulations 1994 (now 1999) – contractual terms relating to the "adequacy" of the contract price are not subject to the general test of fairness in these Regulations.

Facts: The Bank lent money to consumers and a condition of the contract was that:

"Time is of the essence for making all repayments to FNB as they fall due. If any repayment instalment is unpaid for more than seven days after it became due, FNB may serve a notice on the customer requiring payment before a specified date not less than seven days later. If the repayment instalment is not paid in full by that date, FNB will be entitled to demand payment of the balance on the customer's account and interest then outstanding together with all reasonable legal and other costs charges and expenses claimed or incurred by FNB in trying to obtain the repayment of the unpaid instalment of such balance and interest. Interest on the amount which becomes payable shall be charged in accordance with condition 4, at the rate stated in paragraph D overleaf (subject to variation) until payment after as well as before any judgment (such obligation to be independent of and not to merge with the judgment). "

Consumer contacts are subject to the Unfair Terms in Consumer Contracts Regulations which mean that contractual terms in standard form contracts which create a significant imbalance between the consumer and the other party can be challenged as unfair. However, the "fairness" test does not apply to terms which deal with the "adequacy" of the contract price.

Claim: The Director General of Fair Trading objected to the last sentence of this clause, using powers granted under the Regulations, arguing that it was not fair to consumers because it required them to pay interest before and after court judgment in cases where statutory interest would not be payable in the English county courts. The bank argued that the clause dealt with adequacy of price and so was not subject to the "fairness" test at all.

Decision: The House of Lords held that the term in this case did not focus on adequacy but on the appropriateness – or fairness – of including such a clause in these contracts and so its fairness fell to be determined under reg 4 of the 1994 Regulations. It was not part of the core exemption from the "fairness" test. The term was not considered unfair.

Judgment: Lord Bingham said of the term itself at p 20: "It does not concern the adequacy of the interest earned by the bank as its remuneration but is designed to ensure that the bank's entitlement to interest does not come to an end on the entry of judgment."

Thus, it was subject to the "fairness" test, of which he said: "In judging the fairness of the term it is necessary to consider the position of typical parties when the contract is made. The borrower wants to borrow a sum of money, often quite a modest sum, often for purposes of improving his home. He discloses an income sufficient to finance repayment by instalments over the contract term. If he cannot do that, the bank will be unwilling to lend. The essential bargain is that the bank will make funds available to the borrower which the borrower will repay, over a period, with interest. Neither party could suppose that the bank would willingly forgo any part of its principal or interest. If the bank thought that outcome at all likely, it would not lend. If there were any room for doubt about the borrower's obligation to repay the principal in full with interest, that obligation is very clearly and unambiguously expressed in the conditions of contract. There is nothing unbalanced or detrimental to the consumer in that obligation; the absence of such a term would unbalance the contract to the detriment of the lender."

Analysis: A term about post-judgment interest was not concerned with "adequacy" of price and so was subject to the "fairness" test. Had it been to do with adequacy, it would have been exempt from that requirement.

OFT v *Abbey National plc* [2009] UKSC 6

Court: Supreme Court (English case)

Issue: Enforceability of bank charges.

Facts: The Office of Fair Trading ("OFT") challenged the banks on the use of bank charges payable by customers who had gone into overdraft on their current accounts.

Claim: The OFT claimed that such charges were subject to the "fairness" test under the Unfair Terms in Consumer Contracts Regulations 1999 and that they were unfair and therefore not binding on consumers. The banks argued that these charges fell within the definition of clauses exempted from the "fairness" test under the Regulations, namely, that they were to do with "the adequacy of the price or remuneration, as against the goods or services supplied in exchange" under reg 6(2)(b), being a term relating to the adequacy of the price or remuneration and so not subject to the "fairness" test. Regulation 6(2)(b) states: "In so far as it is in plain intelligible language, the assessment of fairness of a term shall not relate— (a) to the definition of the main subject matter of the contract, or (b) to the adequacy of the price or remuneration, as against the goods or services supplied in exchange."

Decision: The Supreme Court found that the contractual term which provided for the charges fell within reg 6(2)(b) and so was not subject to the "fairness" test. It distinguished *Director General of Fair Trading* v *First National Bank* [2002] 1 All ER 97, noting that the interest payable in that case was a payment resulting from breach of contract, not a price or charge made in connection with providing services. In this case, the charges were part of the overall pricing structure for banking services (note – this is because we still have "free personal banking" ie we do not pay a fee each month to run our current accounts but that banking has to be funded through other means).

Judgment: Sir Anthony Clarke MR gave the judgment of the court and at p 90 said:

> "the following considerations are relevant to this broad question, together no doubt with many others, depending upon the facts of the particular case. (i) The nature of the services provided as a whole and the manner and terms in which the standard term documentation is provided to consumers. (ii) The quantum of the particular payment, the goods or services to which it is said to relate and the other payments required under the contract. (iii) In order to be 'price or remuneration' within the meaning of article 4(2) the payment provision must not be ancillary to the central bargain between the consumer and supplier. Along this sliding scale: (a) if the payment obligations are directly negotiated between the consumer and supplier they will not be subject to assessment for fairness under the Directive; (b) the more closely related the payment term is to the essential bargain between the parties, the more likely it is to fall within the exception in article 4(2); but (c) the more ancillary the payment term is and the less likely it is to come to the direct attention of the consumer at the time the contract is entered into, the less likely it is to be within the concept of 'price or remuneration' within the meaning of the Directive."

Analysis: The court found that bank charges fell within the reg 6(2)(b) exemption, relating to adequacy of price or remuneration, and so were not subject to the "fairness" test of the Regulations. These Regulations apply across the UK so this interpretation would be the same in Scotland.

Smith v UMB Chrysler and South Wales Switchgear Ltd 1978 SLT 21

Court: House of Lords (Scottish case)

Issue: Enforceability of an indemnity clause.

Facts: Mr Smith was employed by the South Wales Switchgear Co Ltd (suppliers) and was sent to do work for UMB Chrysler (purchasers) in terms of a contract between UMB Chrysler and South Wales Switchgear which included an indemnity clause which stated: "In the event of this order involving the carrying out of work by the supplier and its subcontractors on land and/or premises of the purchaser, the supplier will keep the purchaser indemnified against

… (b) any liability, loss, claim or proceedings whatsoever under statute or common law (i) in respect of personal injury to or death of any person whomsoever, (ii) in respect of any injury or damage whatsoever to any property real or personal, arising out of or in the course of or caused by the execution of this order …". Mr Smith was injured while working on that job. He sued UMB Chrysler for reparation on the ground that they had been negligent and UMB Chrysler sought to be indemnified by South Wales Switchgear in turn.

Claim: UMB Chrysler as purchasers under the contract with South Wales Switchgear sought to have the indemnity clause enforced so that South Wales Switchgear had to pay it for reparation paid out to Mr Smith. South Wales Switchgear argued that the indemnity clause could not be construed to cover UMB Chrysler's own negligence.

Decision: An indemnity clause should be construed *contra proferentem* (ie against the party seeking to rely on it) and, in this case, it was not sufficiently clear that it was intended to cover the purchaser's own negligence so did not apply in these circumstances.

Judgment: Lord Keith of Kinkel stated at p 16:

> "Certain guidelines of assistance in approaching this task where an exemption clause or a clause of indemnity is under consideration were, however, laid down in the Privy Council case of *Canada Steamship Lines Ltd.* v *The King* [1952] A.C. 192. Lord Morton of Henryton, delivering the advice of the Board, expressed these as follows (at p. 208):—'(1) If the clause contains language which expressly exempts the person in whose favour it is made (hereafter called the "*proferens*") from the consequence of the negligence of his own servants, effect must be given to that provision. … (2) If there is no express reference to negligence, the court must consider whether the words are wide enough, in their ordinary meaning, to cover negligence on the part of the servants of the proferens. If a doubt arises at this point, it must be resolved against the proferens. … (3) If the words are wide enough for the above purpose, the court must then consider whether "the head of damage may be based on some ground other than that of negligence" … The "other ground" must not be so fanciful or remote that the *proferens* cannot be supposed to have desired protection against it; but subject to this qualification … the existence of a possible

head of damage other than that of negligence is fatal to the *proferens* even if the words used are *prima facie* wide enough to cover negligence on the part of his servants. ...'

In *North of Scotland Hydro-Electric Board* v *D. & R. Taylor* 1956 S.C. 1 the Second Division accepted that these principles applied in the law of Scotland. It is to be stressed that they do not represent rules of law, but simply particular applications of wider general principles of construction, the rule that express language must receive due effect and the rule *omnia praesumuntur contra proferentem*. While they apply to the construction both of a clause bearing to exempt from certain liabilities a party who has undertaken to carry out contractual work and of a clause whereby such a party has agreed to indemnify the other party against liabilities which would ordinarily fall upon him, they apply *a fortiori* in the latter case, since it represents a less usual and more extreme situation."

Analysis: An indemnity clause has to be either carefully drafted expressly to include the circumstances the *proferens* wants to rely on or so widely drafted that the circumstance can be deemed to be caught within it or it will not be enforced.

PROBLEMS WITH CONTRACTS:
(vii) ERROR (MISUNDERSTANDING AND MISREPRESENTATION)

Stewart v *Kennedy* (1890) 17 R (HL) 25

Court: House of Lords (Scottish case)

Issue: Could error about the legal context of the contract which was both induced and uninduced affect the contract?

Facts: Mr Stewart owned land which was entailed. Entailment was an old form of land/succession law which limited the sale of land and was designed to keep land in the family (usually for the oldest male heir). However, land could be sold subject to certain formalities being fulfilled, including ratification by the Court of Session. Stewart sold the land to Kennedy subject to "ratification" by the court. Stewart was under the mistaken belief (based on an out-of-date knowledge of the law – beware!) that the court had to approve the price as well as the transfer. In fact, the law had developed so that the court's role was simply to approve the transfer, not the price.

Claim: Mr Stewart wanted the contract reduced on grounds of error; both his own uninduced error but also error induced by Mr Kennedy's agent who had given him the impression that he was correct in the law .

Decision: The court upheld the contract.

Judgment: It was decided that this was not an essential error, not being one of the five listed in Bell's *Principles*, and so did not affect the contract. Lord Watson did, however, go on to say that an uninduced essential error would still not affect an onerous written contract – induced essential error could.

Analysis: As McBryde points out (*McBryde on Contract* (3rd edn), para 15-11), Stewart's assertion that Kennedy's agent also induced his mistaken belief does not seem to have been taken account of in the decision. This case is based on an onerous, written contract: the type of contract that courts are reluctant to interfere with in the law of error. However, there have been other cases in which error has had an effect – see below.

Spook Erection (Northern) Ltd v *Kaye* 1990 SLT 676

Court: Outer House, Court of Session

Issue: Effect of uninduced unilateral error on contract.

Facts: Spook contracted with Kaye to buy property and at the time the contract (called "missives" because this was a sale and purchase of heritable property) was concluded, Kaye thought that the property was subject to a 99-year lease when in fact it was subject to a 990-year lease. This was his mistake: it was not induced by Spook. When this was discovered, he refused to sell.

Claim: Spook sought specific implement (ie asking the court to enforce performance of the missives) and Kaye counter-claimed with a claim to reduce (ie set aside) the missives on the ground that he had entered into them through essential error. Furthermore, he argued that Spook had known that they were under the wrong impression at the time the missives were concluded and that this fact meant that uninduced essential error could be a ground for reduction, contrary to the general rule.

Decision: As a general rule, where a contract has been reduced to formal writing (as missives must be), it cannot be reduced on the ground of uninduced unilateral error alone.

Judgment: Lord Marnoch at p 678 quoted with approval *Gloag on Contract* (2nd edn), at p 440:

> "It is not a sufficient ground for the reduction of a contract that one party gave his assent to it under a mistake. Parties are supposed to inform themselves on points material to their contracts, or to take the consequences if they do not. As it is put by an editor of Bell's *Principles*, if a man "buys too dear or sells too cheap, he is not by reason of his mistake protected from loss'."

Analysis: As a general rule, uninduced unilateral error (however fundamental) cannot be used as the sole ground for reduction of a contract reduced to writing. This case also suggests that *Steuart's Trs v Hart* (1875) 3 R 192 is not binding because it pre-dates *Stewart v Kennedy* (1890) 17 R (HL) 25 in which the law of essential error was clarified so that even uninduced essential error could not affect a written onerous contract. Subsequent case law suggest that the position is different if the other party *takes advantage* of the uninduced error – ie there may be a more subtle "in between" position whereby we have induced error on the one hand, uninduced error on the other hand and a "half-way house" whereby the error is uninduced but taken advantage of – courts may now be more willing to find grounds for challenge there even in onerous written contracts (see *Angus* v *Bryden* 1992 SLT 884 and *Parvaiz* v *Thresher Wines Acquisitions Ltd* 2009 SC 151).

Hunter v *Bradford Property Trust* 1970 SLT 173

Court: House of Lords (Scottish case)

Issue: Error in gratuitous contracts.

Facts: Businesses run by two sisters ran into financial trouble and, to sort matters out, they agreed with creditors to transfer properties to a property trust which would also take on the loans secured over those properties and pay them £8,500. The plan was then for the trust to sell the properties and pay over half of any profit made on the sales to the sisters (ie the price less costs, including repayment of loans and the £8,500 payment already made). This was not properly reflected in the contract: it did not include deduction of costs so meant that the sisters would get half of the *proceeds*, not the *profits*. This was spotted by the trust just before the property auction and the sisters were persuaded to sign a new contract (minute of agreement) reflecting the correct terms, having been told by the trust that they would lose out financially if they did not sign a new contract. The sisters did not understand the strength of their position under contract law.

Claim: The sisters asked the court to reduce (set aside) the second contract on the basis of uninduced essential error on the consequences of failure to sign it. The trust claimed that this written contract was not a gratuitous contract but one based on compromise with reciprocal obligations (which seem to be "You sign or we pull the plug on the sale") and so reduction on this ground was not possible.

Decision: The second agreement was a gratuitous contract and was reduced on the ground of error.

Judgment: Lord President Clyde said at p 176:

> "It is now well settled in the law of Scotland that a person who enters into a gratuitous obligation can reduce the contract if he can establish that he entered into it under essential error. In this respect gratuitous obligations stand in a quite special position. For no such right of reduction would operate in the case of an onerous contract."

He went on:

> "Apart from this aspect of the matter however, I am by no means satisfied that even a pure error in law would bar the reduction of a gratuitous obligation. There is no authority for such a contention in Scotland.
>
> Although an error by one party to an onerous contract where the error is not induced by the other party is not a ground for reducing it (Gloag, *Contract*, p. 452) gratuitous obligations, just because they are gratuitous, are in a different position. In this latter case error by one party may entitle him to reduce it, and in the statement of this proposition in Gloag (*Contract*, p. 453) there is nothing to suggest that the error which can found the reduction of a gratuitous obligation is in any way restricted to an error in fact only. The passage in question would apply

equally to errors of fact or of law. I do not myself consider that the brocard *ignorantia juris haud excusat* would form a relevant defence to an action of reduction of a gratuitous obligation. But it is unnecessary to decide this wider question in the present case for, in my opinion, no question of general principles of law or even of the interpretation of a statutory provision applicable to a large number of cases arises in the present instance. ...

On essential error: The next question is whether, assuming there is error, it was essential. To be essential, the error must be such that but for it the party would have declined to contract. (Lord Watson in *Menzies* v. *Menzies* (1893) 20 R. (HL) 108, at 142). This test is clearly satisfied in the present case. In my opinion therefore the pursuers have made good their case for reduction of the second agreement."

Analysis: This case confirms that gratuitous contracts are treated differently from onerous contracts in cases of essential error. It is also interesting from the point of view of determining when a contract is deemed to be gratuitous.

Steuart's Trs v *Hart* (1875) 3 R 192

Court: Inner House, Court of Session

Issue: Uninduced unilateral error taken advantage of by the other party in an onerous written contract.

Facts: Mr Steuart died, leaving a large plot of land to be sold by his trustees. They sold part of it to Hart. The disposition (transfer of title) to Hart specified that a feu duty of 3s was payable for that part (feu duty being a payment which used to be paid to superiors under the old feudal system). However, the trustees had not meant to apportion the feu duty in this way but to charge the full amount for the plot as a whole (a more substantial £9 15s) to this portion. Hart's agents knew that they had made a mistake when drawing up the disposition but had not said anything.

Claim: Steuart's trustees sought to have the disposition reduced (set aside) on the ground of error or to have the Register of Sasines where the disposition was recorded amended to increase the feu duty to the full amount.

Decision: The court reduced the disposition.

Judgment: The Lord President (Lord Inglis) found that this was an essential error but, more than that, it had been known about and taken advantage of by the purchaser, Hart. It was not competent for the court to amend the Register of Sasines and so reduction was the correct remedy.

Analysis: This case deals with a written onerous contract and the error is deemed to be essential and uninduced but the other party knew about the error and took advantage of it.

Angus v *Bryden* 1992 SLT 884

Court: Outer House, Court of Session

Issue: Error of expression and uninduced error – the court was asked to grant declarator on the construction of missives and rectification of deeds under s 8 of the Law Reform (Miscellaneous Provisions) (Scotland) Act 1985 (error of expression) or, alternatively, to reduce the missives and disposition (transfer of title) on the ground of uninduced error of which the other party had taken advantage.

Facts: The owner of river fishings entered into missives to sell them to an angling club. The missives (contract) referred to the description of the property to be sold found in a disposition (title deed) recorded in 1928 and the seller thought that the missives were only for the *river* fishings referred to in that disposition whereas the purchasers thought that the missives covered all of the fishings included in that disposition, *including* sea fishings. The disposition which was then drafted, signed and recorded to effect the transfer did include *both* river and sea fishings.

Claim: Mr Angus discovered his mistake and sought a declarator that the missives were wrongly drafted and should have included only the river fishings and the subsequent disposition (transfer of title) should be reduced (set aside) He also put forward an *esto* argument (ie an alternative argument based on the court deciding to go the other way): if he was wrong and the court decided that the sea fishings *were* included in the missives then his argument was that they were included by mistake (unintentional error) and the purchasers had taken advantage of his error and the missives and disposition should be reduced on the basis of error.

Decision: Under proper construction, the missives did not include the sea fishings. However, the judge did not reduce the disposition under s 8 of the Law Reform (Miscellaneous Provisions) (Scotland) Act 1985.

Section 8 says (emphasis added):

> "(1) Subject to section 9 of this Act, where the court is satisfied, on an application made to it, that — (a) a document intended to express or to give effect to an agreement fails to express accurately the *common intention* of the *parties to the agreement* at the date when it was made; or (b) a document intended to create, transfer, vary or renounce a right, *not being* a document falling within paragraph (a) above, fails to express accurately the intention of the *grantor* of the document at the date when it was executed, it may order the document to be rectified in any manner that it may specify in order to give effect to that intention."

In this case, the judge considered that the disposition fell into paragraph (a) since it was designed to give effect to the missives and as there was no common intention, it could not be applied to rectify the disposition.

Judgment: Lord Cameron spent much of the judgment considering the issue on error which arose out of the pursuer's alternative argument, so although the case was not decided on the basis of error here, there is a lot of useful opinion on the matter and a useful analysis of cases.

Uninduced error: "… the court is entitled in certain circumstances to go behind a disposition and consider the circumstances in which the missives came to be concluded (*Anderson* v. *Lambie*). The question therefore which properly falls to be considered is whether the pursuer is well founded in asserting that he is entitled to a remedy where there is no inducement to error on the part of the pursuer by the defenders but rather bad faith on the part of the defenders in the sense of taking advantage of that which they know to be an unintended error by the pursuer or, as here, on the part of the pursuer's agents."

For example: "In my opinion, the *ratio* of *Steuart's Trs.* v. *Hart* is that an unintentional error being an error of expression by one party to a contract known to and taken advantage of by the other party is a wrong for which our law provides a remedy, the error being of the nature of essential error, that is, one but for which the party making the error would not have contracted (*Menzies* v. *Menzies*)."

Lord Cameron did not accept the position, adopted in *Spook Erection*, that *Steuart's Trs* was not binding.

Analysis: A case decided on the basis of the proper construction of missives but which also contains useful discussion of uninduced error where one party takes advantage of it.

Parvaiz v *Thresher Wines Acquisitions Ltd* 2009 SC 151

Court: Outer House, Court of Session

Issue: Procedural case about whether to allow proof before answer on case based on alleged error in an auction.

Facts: Mr Parvaiz was interested in buying retail premises which were for sale by auction and he went to view them. He was shown the premises, including toilets situated in a rear extension which were accessed directly from the premises. He bought the premises at auction and paid a 10 per cent deposit which is standard practice. However, he then discovered that the seller did not actually own the toilets – they were not within the seller's title.

Claim: The pursuer, Mr Parvaiz, sought reduction (to have the contract – called minute of preference and enactment of sale in an auction – reduced) and repetition (repayment of the deposit), on the ground of essential error (in this case as to the extent of the premises). The defenders argued, *inter alia*, that the error was uninduced and unilateral and so the contract could not be reduced.

Decision: Proof before answer allowed – the articles of roup (conditions which govern auctions) did not preclude reduction in cases of essential error as to extent of subjects and arguments based on mutual or unilateral error were relevant and could go forward to the next stage of court proceedings

Judgment: There is much discussion of error in this case.

Lord Brodie agreed with counsel who cited McBryde at p 11. His Lordship said: "there are circumstances where in the event of material error in respect of something essential, Scots law allows the remedy of reduction of what on the face of it is a concluded contract. If a rule of thumb were required it would be difficult to improve on Prof McBryde's suggestion that for error to be relevant there must be some other factor in addition. Prof McBryde describes this as 'error plus' (McBryde, para 15.23) …

"Error plus" – *mutual error* at p 18:

"What I understand by that formulation is that McBryde is talking about material error as to the essentials of the contract (of which the subject matter of a contract of sale would be one) and that he takes as a starting point the proposition that one party's error, even if material and essential, will not allow that party to reduce the contract. There must also be something else. A clear example of 'something else' is that the other party was also in error as to the same matter, in other words that there was mutual error ..."

If error unilateral and uninduced at p 20:

"*In Steel's Tr* v. *Bradley Homes (Scotland) Ltd* (p 57) Lord Dunpark notes *dicta* by Lord Reid (p 184) and by Lord President Clyde (p 176) respectively in *Hunter and anr* v. *Bradford Property Trust Ltd* reiterating the general rule that uninduced, unilateral error will not per se found reduction of an onerous contract. Although careful to describe these *dicta* as *obiter* and to point to Lord Watson's apparent allowance for the possibility of exceptional cases in *Stewart* v. *Kennedy* (p 29), Lord Dunpark comes close simply to endorsing the general rule by his observation (p 58) that no such exceptional case has found its way into the law reports. *Steel's Tr* was a case of error as to price. *Royal Bank of Scotland plc* v. *Purvis* was a case of alleged error as to the nature of the contract. In the latter, again without absolutely ruling out the possibility of an exception, Lord McCluskey had difficulty in imagining a case where the general rule would not simply be applied. However, Lord Dunpark's formulation of the general rule is that uninduced, unilateral error will not per se found reduction. His inclusion of 'per se' is suggestive of McBryde's requirement of "error plus'. Here, the "plus', that is the additional factor over and above the pursuer's error, which is relied on by counsel for the pursuer is the possibility, left open by its failure to answer the call at p 10D, that the defender did not act in good faith."

Analysis: This case considers the possibility that a lack of "good faith" on the part of the party not in error may be the additional ingredient which adds up to "error plus" and thus grounds for reduction, although it does not make a decision on it.

Hamilton v *Western Bank* (1861) 23 D 1033

Court: Inner House, Court of Session

Issue: Common essential error.

Facts: The bank sold land to Hamilton with all buildings on it. Both parties were under the mistaken belief that all of the buildings were constructed wholly on the land but, in fact, the boundary was such that some of them were not.

Claim: The parties wanted to have the sale reduced.

Decision: The court agreed.

Judgment: The error as to the extent of the subject-matter of the contract was essential and had been shared by the parties and so the contract was reduced.

Analysis: Common error will render the contract void if essential.

Seaton Brick and Tile Co v *Mitchell* (1900) 2 F 550, (1900) 7 SLT 385

Court: Inner House, Court of Session

Issue: Uninduced unilateral error, with no other factors.

Facts: Mitchell offered to carry out specified carpentry work for £859, and the offer was accepted by Seaton Brick and Tile Co. However, Mitchell refused to go ahead because the written offer had been wrong – it had accidentally missed out some key elements of the job and materials, meaning that the quote was far too low.

Claim: Seaton Brick and Tile Co wanted to claim damages amounting to the difference between the quote and its next best quote (over £300) but Mitchell argued that the contract was flawed as a result of error.

Decision: The court refused to allow Mitchell to resile.

Judgment: The Lord Justice-Clerk said: "The error consists, when examined, in blunders made by his son in making up calculations for him, and thus bringing out the wrong sum, and causing the offer to be made to do the work for a much smaller sum than would have been put down in the offer had these blunders not been made. I am unable to hold that he can legally exempt himself from liability for failure to fulfil his engagements by proving such errors. They were not errors induced by any action of the opposite party. He was supplied with the usual and proper means for estimating for the work, and if he blundered, and by mistakes made in his own office offered to do the work for a sum which would not pay him, *sibi imputet*."

Analysis: This is pure uninduced unilateral error in the contract and did not give a ground for reduction.

Steel's Tr v Bradley Homes (Scotland) Ltd 1972 SC 48

Court: Outer House, Court of Session

Issue: Can uninduced unilateral error result in reduction of contract?

Facts: Mrs Steel contracted with Bradley Homes to sell a piece of land to them. She died and her trustee, Mr Steel, wanted to proceed with the transaction but Bradley refused, saying that there had been a breach of a condition of sale. Mrs Steel's executor raised an action for specific implement but the parties entered into a contract (minute of agreement) agreeing terms of a settlement to drop the case. In it, interest was payable on the settlement sum from 16 March 1971. However, when the amount payable under that contract was being calculated, Mr Steel's solicitor said that there had been a mistake: he had always meant for interest to run from 16 March 1969 and claimed that he had told the other side's solicitors this at the time, which they denied.

Claim: Mr Steel asked the court to grant specific implement of the missives and to reduce the minute of agreement on settlement on the ground of error.

Decision: The parties were bound by the settlement agreement. Uninduced unilateral error did not give rise to grounds for reduction of a written onerous contract.

Judgment: Lord Dunpark said at p 55: "The *Seaton Brick* case vouches a proposition which I believe to be sound and well established in the law of Scotland, namely, that if A offers in writing to perform specified services or deliver specified goods at a stated price, and B, having no reason to believe that A has erroneously understated the price, accepts A's offer in good faith, the contract cannot thereafter be reduced on the ground that A has in fact erroneously understated the price. Is it then possible to reconcile *Sword* v. *Sinclairs* with this proposition? I think that it is."

Note: *Sword* v *Sinclairs* is an old case from 1771 in which an inexperienced apprentice of tea dealers wrote the wrong price against a particular type of tea in a letter (2s 8d instead of the more likely 3s 8d) and then traded with an experienced dealer on the low price. It appears that he was taken advantage of by the older and wiser businessman. The court held that, in this case, the written contract was not enforceable and, in the absence of detailed reasoning to go on, Lord Dunpark went on to discuss its relevance as follows:

> "In the year 1771 the sum of one shilling was substantial, and tea, I believe, was still something of a luxury. I strongly suspect that the Court applied judicial knowledge to the problem and took the view that, whereas 3s. 8d. per pound was a realistic price for tea, 2s. 8d. was not. It is a necessary inference from this view that, in accepting an offer to sell at 2s. 8d. per pound without inquiry, the purchaser did not act in good faith. If this was the *ratio decidendi* of Sword v. Sinclairs—and it may have been, because none is stated—the case would not conflict with the proposition above stated but would illustrate the application of the equitable principle that, where an offer price is so low as to afford reasonable grounds for suspicion that it has been erroneously and substantially understated, the Court may refuse to allow the offeree to take advantage of the offeror's mistake. It may be said that I am not entitled to speculate as to the true *ratio* of Sword v. Sinclairs. So be it. But the fact that the *ratio* is not reported entitles me at least to differ from Gloag's view that the *Seaton Brick* case and *Sword* v. *Sinclairs* are irreconcilable and to treat the latter as an unreliable authority, which I am not bound to follow in this case (see *Great Western Railway Co.* v. *Owners of S.S. Mostyn* [1928] A.C. 57, *per* Viscount Dunedin at p. 73)."

Analysis: A case which emphasises the general rule that written onerous contracts will not be reduced on the ground of unilateral uninduced error. It suggests that there was (in Professor McBryde's term) "error plus" in the old case of *Sword* v. *Sinclairs* and approves the *Seaton Brick* case. Pure uninduced unilateral error is unlikely to result in reduction of an onerous written contract by itself: there must be other factors at play to allow the court to grant reduction.

Ritchie v *Glass* 1936 SLT 591

Court: Outer House, Court of Session

Issue: Alleged essential error in contract.

Facts: Mr Ritchie owned two shops – one double fronted and one single fronted – in Cow Wynd in Falkirk, which he put up for sale. A purchaser saw the advert and collected the schedule of particulars which stated that the frontage of the double shop was about 30 feet and the frontage of the single shop was 15 feet. He instructed Mr Glass, his architect, to make an offer. Missives were concluded. However, when the purchasers measured up the frontage they found that the double-fronted shop measured only just over 21 feet. The purchaser wanted to repudiate the contract straight away.

Claim: Mr Ritchie raised a court action for specific implement against Mr Glass, for performance of the missives. Mr Glass defended the action on the basis that the contract had been entered into on the basis of induced error.

Decision: Implement granted because the error was not material. The particulars had not specified that the frontage alone amounted to the "approximate" figures provided. The fact that the overall total included the entrance to the flat above was not stated in the particulars. Inspection was invited. The figures were an innocent mistake and the purchaser should really have made further inspections.

Judgment: Lord Carston at pp 593 *et seq* made the following comments on whether an induced error has to be essential to result in reduction:

"It has apparently been assumed by some that error, if induced by misrepresentation of the other party to the contract, must also be in regard to an essential – or in substantials – before the contract can be set aside. There seems to me to be no justification for that view in Bell ... It appears clear that Scots law recognises, as indicated by Bell, that when misrepresentation by a party is alleged inducing error in the other in regard to some matter, that matter need not be an essential of the contract, but it must be material and of such a nature that not only the contracting party but any reasonable man might be moved to enter into the contract; or, put the other way, if the misrepresentation had not been made, would have refrained from entering into the contract."

Analysis: Where error is induced, it need not also be an essential error to render the contract challengeable. It has to be material but does not have to be essential. In this case, the induced error was not even material and so the contract stood and could be enforced.

Boyd & Forrest v Glasgow and South-Western Railway Co
1912 SC (HL) 93

Court: House of Lords (Scottish case)

Issue: Effect of misrepresentation on contract, focusing on fraudulent misrepresentation.

Facts: The Glasgow and South-Western Railway Co contracted with Messrs Boyd & Forrest to build a railway branch line for a lump sum of £243,690. Track building requires blasting work and the contract made clear that the contractors, Boyd & Forrest, had to satisfy themselves on the "geology" of it, ie what sort of ground they were dealing with, the strata involved and so on. The railway company had taken bores and also provided a longitudinal section showing their analysis of where the harder material began. However, none of this data was guaranteed and it was very clear that the contractors had to satisfy themselves. It transpired that, in compiling the journal of bores, the railway company's engineer had omitted some details and had edited a couple of entries which he believed genuinely were wrong.

When Boyd & Forrest began work, they found that the strata were much more difficult than they had thought, based on the bore journals and the section provided. Although they knew the full extent of this by the end of 1902, they continued to work and completed the job in 1905 with an extra payment of £10,000. However, they then wanted to be paid what the job had actually cost and not the contract price. A long spell of court action followed.

Claim: The contractors claimed for the extra costs on the basis that they had been induced into the contract by fraudulent misrepresentation. This House of Lords action focused on whether the claims were indeed fraudulent or not.

Decision: No fraud – there had been mix-ups about the terms used for differing types of rock (black ban, black blaes etc) which had caused mistakes to be made in classifying strata as soft or hard but the mistake was innocent.

Judgment: The court found no fraud or recklessness.

Analysis: This is the first of two cases arising out of these circumstances. The railway company then went on to raise an action on the basis of innocent misrepresentation.

Boyd & Forrest v *Glasgow and South-Western Railway Co*
1915 1 SLT 114

Court: House of Lords (Scottish case)

Issue: Second case arising from the facts – this 1915 action centred on whether there had been *innocent* misrepresentation which could be a ground for reduction of contract.

Facts: As for the 1912 action.

Claim: The contractors' position was that the whole contract should be set aside because it had been entered into on the basis of essential error induced by innocent misrepresentation and the work should be paid for on the basis of *quantum meruit* (actual costs).

Decision: The contract could not be reduced because it was not possible to restore the parties to their pre-contractual positions (*restitutio in integrum* being a requirement for reduction in cases of innocent misrepresentation).

Judgment: Earl Lorburn said at p 116:

"Does the law say that when *restitutio in integrum* is impossible, the whole work having been completed two years before the action was commenced, one party to the contract, who has been induced to make it by admittedly innocent representations, can claim damages, and thus in effect substitute for the contract price whatever price the Court may think reasonable? I assume, for argument's sake, that there were, in fact, innocent misrepresentations. I should answer these queries in the negative. I am not, however, writing a treatise on the law, which, indeed, has often been laid down, but deciding the rights of particular litigants. It is enough to say that Messrs Boyd & Forrest knew by the end of 1902 all about certain things. They knew the innocent representations by which they had been induced to make the contract, and they knew the reality about the physical condition of the strata. Knowing both, they elected to proceed and to complete the contract. After that they cannot rely upon the discrepancy between those representations and the reality as a basis of any claim either for rescission or for damages, whether it be called recompense or compensation, or by any other form of words."

On the issue of rescission when *restitutio* is not possible, Lord Shaw of Dunfermline said at p 35:

"... until this case I have not for many years heard it doubted that rescission is not a remedy open to any litigant when matters are not entire and when *restitutio in integrum* is impossible. I do not find myself able fully to comprehend that view of the case which would treat the situation as one equivalent to possible restitution by a process of adjustment of accounts. The railway is there, the bridges are built, the excavations are made, the rails are laid, and the railway itself was in complete working two years before this action was brought. Accounts cannot obliterate it, and unless the railway is obliterated *restitutio in integrum* is impossible ... In the present case *restitutio in integrum* being impossible, I think the law is very well settled, too well and too long settled to be disturbed, as expressed, for instance, by LORD CRANWORTH in *Western Bank of Scotland* v. *Addie*, 'Relief under the first head [ie repudiation or rescission], which is what in Scotland is designated *restitutio in integrum*, can only be had where the party seeking it is able to put those against whom it is asked in the same situation in which they stood when the contract was entered into. Indeed, this is necessarily to be inferred from the very expression *restitutio in integrum*, and the same doctrine is well understood and constantly acted on in England.'"

Analysis: If a contract is proved to have been induced by innocent misrepresentation, then the remedy of reduction or rescission is possible only if *restitutio in integrum* is possible. This contract could not be set aside (reduced) because *restitutio in integrum* was not possible. Damages are not available for innocent misrepresentation (unlike for fraudulent misrepresentation).

Derry v *Peek* (1889) 14 App Cas 337

Court: House of Lords (English case)

Issue: Misrepresentation – fraudulent or not?

Facts: An investor bought shares in Peek's new company on the basis of the share prospectus and the belief that the new company would be allowed to use steam trams when in fact permission was withheld by the regulator, much to the surprise of the company.

Claim: The investor claimed that there had been fraudulent misrepresentation in the prospectus.

Decision: The House of Lords held that the company had not been fraudulent.

Judgment: Lord Herschell stated at p 374: "Fraud is proved when it is shewn that a false representation has been made (1) knowingly, or (2) without belief in its truth or (3) recklessly, careless whether it be true or false."

Analysis: This definition of fraudulent misrepresentation has been accepted into Scots law – see the *Boyd & Forrest* cases.

Esso Petroleum Co Ltd v *Mardon* [1976] QB 801

Court: Court of Appeal (English case)

Issue: Negligent misrepresentation.

Facts: Mr Mardon leased a petrol station from Esso on the basis of their projected throughput of 200 000 gallons of petrol per year. In fact, as the petrol station had to be built in such a way as to comply with planning regulations which obscured the pumps from the road, it was used much less than that, but Esso did not revise its predictions and insisted that the estimated throughput was realistic. In the end, Mr Mardon was losing money and eventually could not pay his bills. Esso cut off his supplies; he left.

Claim: Esso claimed for return of the premises and monies owing. Mr Mardon counter-claimed for breach of warranty, failing which reduction of the contract on the ground of negligent misrepresentation.

Decision: Breach of warranty claim upheld, there was also negligent misrepresentation by Esso whose "servant" had been held out as an expert in the matter and so owed a duty of care to Mr Mardon.

Judgment: Lord Denning said at p 819: "It seems to me that *Hedley Byrne & Co. Ltd.* v *Heller & Partners Ltd.* [1964] A.C. 465, properly understood, covers this particular proposition: if a man, who has or professes to have special knowledge or skill, makes a representation by virtue thereof to another – be it advice, information or opinion – with the intention of inducing him to enter into a contract with him, he is under a duty to use reasonable care to see that the representation is correct, and that the advice, information or opinion is reliable. If he negligently gives unsound advice or misleading information or expresses an erroneous opinion, and thereby induces the other side to enter into a contract with him, he is liable in damages."

Analysis: English case in which negligent misrepresentation inducing contract can result in reduction if duty of care owed by the party making the misrepresentation to the party seeking to rely on it. Note: s 10 of the Law Reform (Miscellaneous Provisions) (Scotland) Act 1985 applies in Scotland:

Hamilton v *Allied Domecq plc* 2007 SC (HL) 142

Court: House of Lords (Scottish case)

Issue: Could non-disclosure (ie silence) on an issue amount to negligent misstatement?

Facts: Mr Hamilton and another party invested in a company to exploit the bottled water market through developing springs at Gleneagles estate. They needed a business partner to do this and so entered into a contract with Allied. Allied's representative, Mr Beatty, knew how Mr Hamilton *et al* wanted to market and distribute the new brand but did not say that the method of distribution to be used at his end would be different. The distribution method was not covered in the contract (subscription agreement in this case).

Claim: Mr Hamilton and others claimed either that the representative had a "duty to speak" or that he had negligently misrepresented the facts.

Decision: There was no evidence of misrepresentation.

Judgment: Lord Rodger of Earlsferry said: "Counsel for the appellants accepted that something more than mere silence would usually be required to found a delictual claim for damages, but he argued that in certain circumstances a duty to speak would arise. In such cases a failure to speak would be negligent in law and a claim for damages could arise. For support, he pointed to the passage in the decision of the Court of Appeal in *Banque Keyser Ullmann SA* v. *Skandia (UK) Insurance Co Ltd* (pp 794H–795A) where Slade LJ said:

'We can see no sufficient reason on principle or authority why a failure to speak should not be capable of giving rise to liability in negligence under *Hedley Byrne* principles, provided that the two essential conditions are satisfied.'

Slade LJ had already identified the two essential conditions as being 'that there has been on the facts a voluntary assumption of responsibility in the relevant sense and reliance on that assumption.' He added (p 794E–F): 'These features may be much more difficult to infer in a case of mere silence than in a case of misrepresentation.'

23 [23] My Lords, the simple truth is that counsel for the appellants was unable to point to anything in the facts or evidence to show that, in this particular commercial negotiation, there had been any voluntary assumption of responsibility on the part of Mr Beatty. Nor have I been able to find any. In these circumstances the *Banque Keyser* decision does not provide a basis for holding that Mr Beatty was under a duty of care to tell Mr Hamilton about the defenders' distribution strategy if it differed from the one favoured by Mr Hamilton. Counsel for the appellants did not suggest that such a duty could be founded on anything other than a voluntary assumption of responsibility. The alternative way of putting the pursuers' case must therefore be rejected. So, if they are to succeed, it can only be on the basis that there was a negligent misrepresentation by Mr Beatty."

Analysis: There is no general positive "duty to speak" but if one party has assumed a duty of care to the other then silence can amount to misrepresentation. In this case, there was no such assumption of duty and so the contract stood.

*Raffle*s v *Wichelhaus* (1864) 2 H & C 906

Court: English Court of Exchequer

Issue: Did error about the subject-matter affect the contract where both parties were in error?

Facts: Two parties contracted for the transport of cotton from Bombay on a ship called *Peerless*. Unfortunately, there were two ships of the same name and so the parties were at cross purposes – each thinking about a different ship and sailing time, one in October and one in December.

Claim: The buyers refused to take delivery of the cotton which had sailed on the December *Peerless* and the sellers claimed the contract price.

Decision: The court held that there was no contract.

Judgment: The court found that the error was essential and went to the heart of the contract, meaning that there was no *consensus in idem* and so the contract was void.

Analysis: Where parties are both in error, there is more likely to be a lack of consensus than if only one of them has made a mistake.

Morrisson v *Robertson* 1908 SC 332

Court: Inner House, Court of Session

Issue: Can essential error about identity make a contract void or voidable?

Facts: Telford tricked a man, Mr Morrisson, into selling two cows to him on credit, by pretending to be the son of a man with whom Morrisson had done business before and who he knew to be good for credit. Telford then sold the cows on to an innocent third party, Mr Robertson. Mr Morrison sued Mr Robertson for the return of the cows or, failing that, the price.

Claim: Mr Morrisson claimed that the cows should be returned to him because he had parted with them either as a result of theft or as a result of essential error, making Telford's title to them *void*. Mr Robertson argued that he had bought them from Telford who had a *voidable* title to the cows and not a void title and because the contract between Morrisson and Telford had not been avoided (ie set aside) by the time he bought the cows in good faith, they were his to keep.

Judgment: Lord M'laren said at p 701:

"It is perfectly plain that in such circumstances there was no contract between Telford and the pursuer, because Telford did not propose to buy the cows for himself, and because the pursuer would not have sold them on credit to a man of whom he had no knowledge. Neither was there any sale of the cows by the pursuer to Mr Wilson, Bonnyrigg [the man who Telford pretended was his father]. Wilson knew nothing about them, and never authorised the purchase: the whole story was an invention. There being no sale either to Wilson or to Telford, and there being no other party concerned in the business in hand, it follows that there was no contract of sale at all, and there being no contract of sale the pursuer remained the undivested owner of his cows, although he had parted with their custody to Telford in consequence of these false representations.

So much being premised, then I think it follows that as Telford had no right to the cows he could not give a good title to the defender even under a contract for an onerous consideration. He had no better title to sell the cows to any third person than he would have had if he had gone into the pursuer's byre and stolen the cows. This seems to me to be perfectly clear upon a consideration of known principles, but it is satisfactory that in the judgment which we are to give according to the law of Scotland, we are confirmed by a decision of the English Court of Exchequer, in circumstances which are in all respects parallel to those in the present case – I mean the case of *Higgons* v *Burton*, 1857, 26 L.J. Ex. 342."

Analysis: The essential error about the identity of the purchaser rendered the original "contract" void so it never had an effect, no legal consequences could flow from it, the cows were still Morrisson's and the best Robertson could hope for was to track down Telford and get his money back. Contrast with *Macleod* v *Kerr* below.

Shogun Finance Ltd v *Hudson* [2004] 1 AC 919

Court: House of Lords (English case)

Issue: Is identity of the "consumer" essential in a consumer credit transaction?

Facts: Mr Hudson bought a car from a man who had obtained the car on hire purchase from Shogun Finance Ltd by pretending to be Mr Patel, a man who had a good credit rating. He had defrauded Shogun by producing Mr Patel's driving licence (which had been "improperly obtained") which they had used to run a credit check.

Claim: Mr Hudson claimed that he had good title to the car under s 27 of the Hire Purchase Act 1964 which offers protection to *bona fide* third-party (private) purchasers and allows for the effective transfer of title from the hiree under the HP contract to an innocent third party. Shogun Finance Ltd argued that the original HP agreement was void because of the fraudulent misrepresentation of the man pretending to be Mr Patel.

Decision: The car belonged to Shogun Finance Ltd and so Mr Hudson could not obtain good title to the car. The parties to the HP contract referred to in s 27 of the 1964 Act were Shogun Finance Ltd and Mr Patel. Mr Patel had not consented to the contract and so it was void. The innocent third party therefore did not obtain the protection of s 27.

Judgment: In a majority decision, three of the Law Lords decided that the issue of who had contracted with Shogun fell to be decided as a matter of construction. Although dissenting opinion was that the face-to-face negotiations meant that Shogun had contracted with the "rogue" (whatever he chose to call himself), the contract stated that it was between Mr Patel and Shogun: Mr Patel had never authorised the contract and so it was void.

Analysis: The issue of identity is still an area in which essential error can void a contract. This case was followed in another English case recently, in *TTMI Sarl* v *Statoil ASA* [2011] EWHC 1150 (Comm) in which brokers referred to the wrong company when negotiating a contract for charter of a ship. The correspondence named Sempra, the parent company, as the owner rather than its subsidiary, TTMI, on the one side and Statoil on the other. The court looked to the terms of the contract to determine the contractual parties. Ultimately, this case was decided on the conduct of the parties but the case of *Shogun* was used to highlight the importance of who is contracting, especially when this is written down.

Macleod v *Kerr* 1965 SC 253

Court: First Division, Inner House, Court of Session

Issue: Another fraudulent misrepresentation case – was the fact that the purchaser of a car gave a false name to the seller enough to render the contract void?

Facts: Mr Kerr owned a car which he sold to Mr Galloway (who gave his name as Mr Craig at the time). The purchaser paid for the car with a stolen cheque which bounced. The "rogue" then sold the car on to Mr Gibson. Mr Kerr informed the police and they traced the car to Mr Gibson and removed it from him. Mr Galloway, the rogue, was later convicted for fraud and theft of the car.

Claim: An action for multiplepoinding was raised to determine who owned the car. In an earlier hearing, the sheriff substitute had found that the car was stolen and so title had never passed to Galloway to be able to pass it on. Mr Gibson argued that this was not the case: the original contract was voidable, not void.

Decision: The car had not been stolen because Mr Kerr had intended to transfer title (so the definition of theft was not met). Thus the contract between Mr Kerr and Mr Galloway was not void. It was, however, voidable for fraudulent misrepresentation and capable of being rescinded. It was not rescinded in time to prevent transfer of title from Galloway to Gibson. Thus, Gibson had title.

Judgment: This case differs from *Morrisson* because Mr Kerr intended to contract with the person in front of him (whatever his name). In *Morrisson*, the identity of the purchaser was all important. Here, the fraud which affected the contract was in the payment by stolen cheque. The failure of Mr Kerr to avoid the contract before the sale on to the innocent third party meant that Mr Gibson acquired good title. Professor T B Smith's critique of the decision in *Morrisson* was itself criticised by Lord President Clyde: Professor Smith had argued that *Morrisson* had been a case of theft and not error but, for the same reason as he gave in this case, the Lord President highlighted that theft cannot occur when goods are handed over voluntarily. He confirmed the *ratio* in *Morrisson* as correct.

Analysis: This case confirms that one must be careful to determine what it is that undermines the contract because cause and effect can lead to very different outcomes.

Wilson v *Marquis of Breadalbane* (1859) 21 D 957

Court: Inner House, Court of Session

Issue: Error as to price.

Facts: Two men traded cows; Wilson thought that he was selling at £15 per head and the Marquis thought that he was buying at £13 per head. The contract was carried out.

Claim: The court action was to determine the price.

Decision: The court held that there was a valid contract even although the essential element of the price had not been agreed. The parties had acted on the contract and so it stood.

Judgment: The court seems to have emphasised the fact that the parties themselves had changed the position by acting on the contract and that if the court action had arisen before the contract as executed, the decision would have been that there was a lack of consensus. As it was, the court specified the price as the value which was £15 per head.

Analysis: This case is a good example of the fact that contracts need to be challenged before they are fulfilled. Even essential error as to price could not render it void post fulfilment.

Royal Bank of Scotland plc v *Purvis* 1990 SLT 262

Court: Outer House, Court of Session

Issue: Whether uninduced error as to the legal content of a contract rendered it void.

Facts: Mr and Mrs Purvis signed a contract when visiting their bank. Mrs Purvis thought it had something to do with their house purchase but it was actually a guarantee for money lent to Mr Purvis for business. She was a director of the company but took nothing to do with the business.

Claim: Mrs Purvis argued that she had not known what was in the deed she was signing. This error undermined the transaction and the guarantee was void through essential error: she had not intended to act as guarantor and so there was no consensus.

Decision: The contract of guarantee was binding on both Mr and Mrs Purvis.

Judgment: Lord McCluskey reiterated the principle that although consensus is indeed required for the formation of contract and essential error can bar formation, once the contract is written down, the court will not look at the intentions of the parties in cases of uninduced error.

Analysis: Just as ignorance of the law is no excuse, failure to read contracts before signing them does not release the parties from obligations created thereby.

PROBLEMS WITH CONTRACTS:
(viii) OTHER PREJUDICIAL CIRCUMSTANCES (FACILITY AND CIRCUMVENTION, UNDUE INFLUENCE, FORCE AND FEAR, GOOD FAITH, SPOUSAL GUARANTEES)

MacGilvary v Gilmartin 1986 SLT 89

Court: Outer House, Court of Session

Issue: What constitutes facility and circumvention or undue influence to allow a contract formed in such circumstances to be set aside (reduced)?

Facts: Mrs MacGilvary's husband died and, soon after, her daughter had her sign a disposition of her house on the Isle of Luing over to her. The exact facts about where and when the disposition was signed were not clear to Mrs MacGilvary and no specific instances of fraud or deceitful behaviour were averred in her case. It had been Mrs MacGilvary's intention to leave that house to her son and the family was aware of that wish.

Claim: Mrs MacGilvary asked the court to set aside the disposition. The defender argued that the case should not proceed because of a lack of relevance and specification in Mrs MacGilvary's pleadings (the written case presented to the court).

Decision: The court did not require specific evidence of deceitful behaviour or undue influence to be able to decide such a case and so the lack of such allegations did not undermine the relevance and specification of the claims.

Judgment: The fact that a person is in a facile condition (for example, recently bereaved and frail as a result) or that there is a relationship between two parties which could open up the possibility of undue influence was all that was required to proceed: proof of deceit was not required.

Analysis: A case involving fraud would require such evidence but facility and circumvention and undue influence are very much focused on the state of health of the person seeking to rely on it and on the relationship between the parties respectively.

Gray v *Binny* (1879) 7 R 332

Court: Inner House, Court of Session

Issue: Undue influence.

Facts: A son was persuaded by his mother to make a bad bargain over his inheritance in which he was disentailed for a sum much lower than the value of the property in question.

Claim: After his mother's death, Mr Gray sought to have the transaction reduced.

Decision: The disentailment was reduced.

Judgment: The court found that the relationship between the mother and son meant that she exerted parental influence. Parental influence could result in undue influence.

Analysis: This case introduced the doctrine of undue influence into Scots law.

Honeyman's Exrs v *Sharp* 1978 SC 223 (aka *Rodgers* v *Sharp*)

Court: Outer House, Court of Session

Issue: To what category of relationships does the doctrine of undue influence extend?

Facts: Mrs Honeyman owned an art collection and, following the death of her husband, had it valued by art dealers in connection with a possible sale. She developed a working relationship with one of the dealers, Mr Sharp, who advised her on her collection and she discussed her will with him and took him into her confidence on a range of matters. He also gave Mrs Honeyman advice and became a friend and support when she fell ill. When Mrs Honeyman died from cancer, he said that she had given him four valuable paintings before she died and had a signed note from her purporting to gift them to him as her "friend".

Claim: Mrs Honeyman's executors claimed that the gift should be reduced (set aside) because it had been made under the *undue influence* of Mr Sharp. Mr Sharp claimed that the doctrine of undue influence did not apply to advisers in his type of role.

Decision: The court held that undue influence did not apply only to those in known positions of trust such as solicitors but to anyone who undertook a professional advisory role and came to be relied upon by the advisee. However, in such cases, the rules would be applied more strictly than for the known categories of relationship.

Judgment: The Lord Ordinary agreed that the list of advisers and persons to whom undue influence applies is not closed and that it could apply to an art dealer or other specialist who gives advice. His Lordship also commented that undue influence requires that the trust placed in that adviser has been abused for the adviser's own benefit: fraud and deceit need not necessarily be involved.

Analysis: There are a number of grounds on which a transaction can be set aside because of the circumstances surrounding it and undue influence is the most relevant where there is an advisory relationship in which the adviser has the trust of the other but abuses it for their own advantage. It is separate from but may be found alongside "facility and circumvention" in which the frailty of one person is taken advantage of by another. Fraud is not a pre-requisite for a case of undue influence – indeed, if there is fraud then that would seem to fall more squarely in the fraudulent misrepresentation category.

Earl of Orkney v *Vinfra* (1606) Mor 1648

Court: Court of Session

Issue: Effect of force and fear on contract.

Facts: The Earl used a threat of violence to induce signature of the contract.

Claim: The contract should be reduced.

Decision: The contract was void.

Judgment: Force and fear can remove consent and render the contract void.

Analysis: Force and fear removes consent in cases of physical violence or threats thereof.

Allen v *Flood* [1898] AC 1 (aka *Flood* v *Jackson*)

Court: House of Lords (English case)

Issue: Effect of economic pressure on contract.

Facts: Boilermakers objected to the employment of shipwrights to carry out iron work on a ship repair contract and threatened to walk out if the shipwrights were not dismissed. Their employers knew that any such action would have dire financial consequences and after a meeting with the boilermaker society's representative, Mr Allen, they relented and sacked the shipwrights.

Claim: The dismissed men raised an action against the boilermakers' society representative for maliciously inducing the employers to breach their contract of employment and intimidating and coercing them not to offer new contracts.

Decision: It was held that the employers had not been "intimidated and coerced" into making their decision.

Judgment: The court was split, with three Law Lords dissenting, but, ultimately, the majority view was that the action taken here by the boilermaker society's representative could not be compared with the highwayman holding a pistol to the head of a traveller. Accordingly, the decision to sack the men (which was lawful at the time because of the type of casual contract they were on) was not rendered unlawful by the action of Mr Allen.

Analysis: This case demonstrates that economic pressure cannot usually be equated to "force and fear" which would be a ground for challenging any contract or other act.

Smith v Bank of Scotland 1997 SC (HL) 111

Court: House of Lords (Scottish case)

Issue: Can misrepresentation by a third party affect a gratuitous contract of caution?

Facts: Mrs Smith signed a standard security over the family home to secure the business debts of her husband. She had no direct interests in the business. This meant that Mrs Smith was cautioner (a Scots term for "guarantor") for her husband's business and thus the standard security was a contract of caution (pronounced "cayshun"). Special rules apply to contracts of caution because they involve three parties: the creditor, the debtor and the cautioner. The contract is between the creditor and the cautioner but covers the debtor's obligations.

Claim: Mrs Smith asked the court partially to reduce the security (ie have it set aside) on the ground of misrepresentation by her husband (induced error). Mrs Smith claimed that the standard security should be reduced because she had signed it following misrepresentations by her husband and had not received any independent legal advice. In other words, Mrs Smith sought to have a contract of caution between herself and the bank set aside on the ground of misrepresentation by a third party, her husband.

Decision: Mrs Smith was successful.

Judgment: The court found that the general law on contracts of caution is that the creditor (in this case, the bank) must be fair in presenting information to the cautioner but the cautioner is obliged to take care of his own business. However, the English case of *Barclays* v *O'Brien* had been decided at this stage in which it was held that the fact that the two parties who take the role of debtor and cautioner (or English equivalent) were cohabiting, puts the creditor on constructive notice of an increased risk of both undue influence and misrepresentation occurring. This resulted in English law extending the law in favour of guarantors/cautioners. Lord Clyde said that the court had to decide whether the same should happen in Scots law since the two had been developing along similar lines up until this case. His Lordship found that it should but for different reasons because the English case of *O'Brien* depended on the English doctrine of notice and also a presumption of undue influence in cases involving spouses, neither of which are features of Scots law. Instead, Lord Clyde argued at p 121 that the same result could be achieved in Scots law by underpinning the decision with the doctrine of good faith required in contracts of caution. That element of good faith is limited and restricted but where a creditor "reasonably suspects" that the relationship between the cautioner spouse and the debtor spouse may be such that it affects the validity of the contact then that narrow duty of good faith would arise and steps should be taken to discharge that obligation to the cautioner by giving advice.

Analysis: This case has been criticised for extending the duty of good faith. See the case of *Royal Bank of Scotland plc* v *Wilson* below.

Royal Bank of Scotland plc v *Wilson* 2004 SC 153, 2003 SLT 910

Court: Inner House, Court of Session

Issue: Another spousal guarantee case.

Facts: Two couples granted standard securities in favour of the bank: one couple were Francis and Annette Wilson and the other were John and Norma Wilson. The men were brothers. The standard securities were granted in connection with a house purchase and building a conservatory respectively. They were "all sums" securities: the personal bond element stated that they would repay "all sums of principal, interest and charges which are now and which may at any time hereafter become due to the Bank by the Obligant whether solely or jointly with any other person, corporation, firm or other body and whether as principal or surety".

This is fairly standard practice. Later on, the brothers entered into loan agreements with the bank for their two business partnerships and defaulted on the loans. The wives had no direct interests in the businesses. The bank tried to recover the business loans from the firms and the brothers themselves but they defaulted so the bank decide to enforce the standard securities.

Claim: The bank tried to enforce the standard securities in respect of these business debts and the wives argued that the cautionary obligations contained in the standard securities ("sureties" in the language of the securities) were not enforceable as they had been misled in to believing that the securities were for the original home loans only, not the business debts.

Decision: The court decided in favour of the bank. It held that the securities here were not gratuitous cautionary obligations and no relevant defences of misrepresentation and bad faith had been pleaded.

Judgment: Lord Justice-Clerk Gill had to decide whether the securities were gratuitous cautionary obligations in the first place. His Lordship held that the securities were cautionary so far as the business debts were concerned since the "all sums" nature allowed the debts of a third party (ie the firms and the brothers as partners of the firms) to be added, turning the wives into cautioners for those debts. However, his Lordship decided that they did not fall into the category of *gratuitous* obligations because they had been granted for loans made to both spouses in each couple in the first place and the all sums wording meant that each spouse was as liable as the other. He noted at p 24 that the security in the *Smith* case had also been an "all sums" security but that this point was not raised in that case but found it "decisive" in this case. His Lordship goes on to note that no specific "actionable wrong" (in this case, act of misrepresentation by the husbands) had been put forward by the defenders. The judgment notes that the Scottish case of *Smith* achieved the same ends as the English case of *Barclays* v *O'Brien* but by different means: not by the English doctrine of constructive notice but by extending the doctrine of good faith. Lord Justice-Clerk Gill said at p 29: "In my opinion, the principle of good faith implies no more than that the creditor ought not to take such a security from the wife where, on an objective judgment of the circumstances, he has reason to think that the wife's consent to grant it may have been vitiated by misrepresentation, undue influence or some other wrongful act committed by her husband."

Analysis: This case has given rise to much court action, the latest of which culminated in a Supreme Court case decided on the interpretation of, *inter alia*, s 19 of the Conveyancing and Feudal Reform (Scotland) Act 1970 and enforcement procedures of standard securities but this Court of Session case focused on the basic issue of enforceability of spousal guarantees. The decision that "all sums" securities are not gratuitous is important since their use is standard practice and so there will be few cases where a spousal guarantee is truly gratuitous, thus invoking special protections. Furthermore, by putting the onus on the cautioner spouse to show an actionable wrong on the part of the debtor spouse (eg actual misrepresentation), the gateway to challenge has been narrowed further still.

CONTRACTUAL TERMS

Spurling v *Bradshaw* [1956] 2 All ER 121

Court: Court of Appeal (English case)

Issue: Enforceability of an exemption clause in a contract.

Facts: A sent eight barrels of orange juice to a warehouse to be stored but when A got them back, the barrels were damaged and/or empty. The contract sent over a few days after the orange juice had been delivered contained small print referring to conditions on the back which included the "London lighterage clause" – an exemption clause which exempted the warehousemen from loss and damage caused by their negligence, wrongful acts etc.

Claim: A refused to pay the bill for the warehousing, the warehousemen sued for their contract price and A counter-claimed for damages for breach of contract on the ground that the warehousemen had failed to take reasonable care which was an implied term in the contract.

Decision: The exemption clause had been incorporated (there was sufficient notice of it) and it was valid and so exempted the warehousemen from liability.

Judgment: Lord Denning agreed with *Parker* (below) at p 466: "I quite agree that the more unreasonable a clause is, the greater the notice which must be given of it. Some clauses which I have seen would need to be printed in red ink on the face of the document with a red hand pointing to it before the notice could be held to be sufficient. The clause in this case, however, in my judgment, does not call for such exceptional treatment, especially when it is construed, as it should be, subject to the proviso that it only applies when the warehouseman is carrying out his contract, and not when he is deviating from it or breaking it in a radical respect."

Analysis: Lord Denning's words were referred to in *Interfoto Picture Library Ltd* v *Stiletto Visual Programmes Ltd* [1989] QB 433 as a fair summary of the law.

Parker v *South-Eastern Railway Co* (1876–77) LR 2 CPD 416

Court: Court of Appeal (English case)

Issue: Incorporation of terms of contract in ticket case.

Facts: Mr Parker deposited his bag in a railway cloakroom, paid the fee and received a ticket which stated on the front "See back". On the back, the ticket stated that the railway company would not be liable for any package exceeding a certain sum. A sign with the same message was hung on the cloakroom wall. The bag disappeared and as its value exceeded the maximum stated on the ticket, the railway company refused to compensate Mr Parker.

Claim: Mr Parker claimed that the exclusion clause had not been validly incorporated – he had assumed that it was simply a receipt for the bag and had not read it. This case had to decide whether there had been a misdirection in the prior trial and whether a new trial should be arranged.

Decision: The court decided that there should be a new trial. The issue was not whether the person has *read* the ticket but whether he saw writing on it and knew or believed that this contained conditions.

Judgment: The court (especially Mellish LJ) found that the key test is about notice, not whether it has been read – if the person seeking to argue against incorporation knew there was written matter and that it concerned the present transaction, and therefore themselves, they had been put on notice as though the porter had said: "Read that, it concerns the matter in hand" (Bramwell LJ at p 428).

Analysis: This important case set the test of notice for incorporation in tickets and the test laid down by Mellish LJ was approved in the House of Lords case *Richardson* v *Rowntree* [1894] AC 217. Its application in Scotland can be found in *Williamson* v *North of Scotland and Orkney Steam Navigation Co* 1916 SC 554 – see below.

Interfoto Picture Library Ltd v *Stiletto Visual Programmes Ltd*
[1989] QB 433, [1988] 1 All ER 348

Court: Court of Appeal (English case)

Issue: Incorporation and notice of unusual or onerous terms.

Facts: Interfoto were a photographic transparencies library and hired out transparencies. Stiletto had never used them before but took out 47 transparencies to use and returned them after 4 weeks. Interfoto then invoiced Stiletto for more than £3,500 as a "holding charge" because Stiletto had had the transparencies longer than 14 days and according to Interfoto had run up a charge of £5 per day per transparency under the terms of the contract which they argued was set out in the delivery note sent with the transparencies. That note read:

> "All transparencies must be returned to us within 14 days from the date of posting/delivery/collection. A holding fee of £5 plus VAT per day will be charged for each transparency which is retained by you longer than the said period of 14 days save where a copyright licence is granted or we agree a longer period in writing with you."

Condition 8 stated:

> "When sent by post/delivered/collected the above conditions are understood to have been accepted unless the package is returned to us immediately by registered mail or by hand containing all the transparencies whole and undefaced and these conditions shall apply to all transparencies submitted to you whether or not you have completed a request form."

Stiletto refused to pay.

Claim: Interfoto sued for the full amount, based on a contractual right to the holding fee. Stiletto argued, *inter alia*, that the £5 per day charge was unusual and onerous and more should have been done to draw their attention to it.

Decision: The court found in favour of Stiletto.

Judgment: The Court of Appeal agreed with the lower court that a fair and reasonable charge would have been £3.50 per transparency per week and so the charge of £5 per day was unusual and onerous. That being so, the authorities of *Parker* and *Spurling* had to be applied and insufficient notice was given to incorporate this clause into the contract.

Analysis: Reiterates the key issue about notice and was applied most recently in *Ryanair Ltd* v *Billigfluege.de GmbH* [2010] IEHC 47, [2010] ILPr 22 (HC (Irl)). Incidentally, the court did not award Interfoto nothing: they were awarded a sum based on *quantum meruit*, ie the reasonable sum for the charge (£3.50 per transparency per week).

Taylor v *Glasgow Corp* 1952 SC 440

Court: Inner House, Court of Session

Issue: A Scottish case on adequate notice for incorporation of terms into contract (public baths case).

Facts: Mrs Taylor went to the public baths at Woodside, paid for a hot bath and received a ticket which had the words "For conditions see other side" printed in legible characters on the front. On the back – again, in legible characters – was "The Corporation of Glasgow are *not* responsible for any loss, injury or damage sustained by persons entering or using this establishment or its equipment". This legend was printed in a continuous strip along all tickets so some had parts of the sentence before or after it. Mrs Taylor injured herself through alleged negligence on the part of Glasgow Corporation.

Claim: Mrs Taylor claimed damages in delict but Glasgow Corporation argued that the contract contained a valid exclusion clause which excluded liability and so it did not have to pay (this case pre-dates the Unfair Contract Terms Act 1977 etc). It argued that the "ticket cases" meant that the fact that notice was given on the front of the ticket meant that the clause on the back was properly incorporated into the contract. The lower courts found in favour of Mrs Taylor and the Corporation appealed the finding.

Decision: The Court of Session found in favour of Mrs Taylor.

Judgment: Lord Justice-Clerk Thomson noted that tickets have many functions and so one could not simply assume that all "ticket cases" are the same. The background and circumstances had still to be taken into account and, in this case, the condition was not validly incorporated into the contract.

Analysis: Be careful not to assume that the important thing in these cases is the name of the piece of paper – not all "ticket cases" have the same outcome. Although it is well settled that transport tickets with "See back for conditions" or similar will incorporate terms effectively, the purpose of the "ticket" and background circumstances should always be considered.

Williamson v North of Scotland and Orkney Steam Navigation Co
1916 SC 554

Court: Inner House, Court of Session (Bench of Five Judges)

Issue: Incorporation of terms into contract when the clause in question was in tiny print.

Facts: Mr Williamson was injured as he disembarked from the company's steam ship at Shetland and he argued that the injury was caused by its negligence. The ticket he had been given was about the size of a normal rail ticket and had a clause on the front which purported to exclude liability: the court noted a shortened version of it as: "The Company is not liable for any injury ... to passengers ... by negligence of their servants." It was in the tiniest print available and there was nothing to draw attention to it (eg a heading, a hand pointing to it etc).

Claim: Mr Williamson claimed for his injury and the defenders argued that liability had been excluded effectively (again, a pre-Unfair Contract Terms Act 1977 case).

Decision: The Court of Session found in favour of Mr Williamson and disagreed that the clause had been incorporated into the contract.

Judgment: The court agreed that the *locus classicus* can be found in *Parker* in Mellish LJ's judgment which contained the rules or principles upon which decisions in this area should be made, as approved in *Richardson* v *Rowntree.*

Analysis: In this case, the exclusion clause was on the front of the ticket, not referred to on the back, but that in itself was not adequate notice because of the tiny print used and no other distinguishing features drawing attention to the clause itself. So, notice requires more than simply being placed on the front of a ticket.

Thornton v *Shoe Lane Parking Ltd* [1971] 2 QB 163

Court: Court of Appeal (English case)

Issue: The incorporation of express terms into a contract in which the term was printed on a car parking ticket issued after the driver had entered the car park.

Facts: The plaintiff, Mr Thornton, entered a multi-storey car park with automatic ticketing of the sort that we are all familiar with today but which was quite novel in 1970. He had not visited it before. There was a notice outside which said "All Cars Parked At Owner's Risk". A ticket was issued automatically by a machine at the entrance when Mr Thornton put his money in. The ticket referred to the conditions of use: eight lengthy conditions were posted on a pillar near the ticket machine and one of these conditions stated that the defendants would not be liable for any injury to the customer occurring when his car was on the premises. When Mr Thornton later collected the car, there was an accident in which he was severely injured and he was awarded damages by a lower court.

Claim: The defendants, Shoe Lane Parking, appealed this decision, arguing that it was exempt from liability due to the incorporation of an exclusion clause in the contract (ie it was not liable for personal injury). This case pre-dates the Unfair Contract Terms Act 1977 and so the protections in that Act for consumers did not exist: such a clause could be enforceable even for personal injury sustained where the defendant was at fault. Mr Thornton's argument rested on the premise that the exclusion term had not been validly incorporated into the contract. Lord Denning summarised the facts surrounding the ticket.

Decision: The contract had been concluded when the plaintiff, Mr Thornton, put the money in the slot of the ticket machine and so the exclusion clause was not incorporated into the contract because it was referred to post conclusion of contract, ie too late.

Judgment: Lord Denning was referred to earlier "ticket cases" but said:

> "none of those cases has any application to a ticket which is issued by an automatic machine. The customer pays his money and gets a ticket. He cannot refuse it. He cannot get his money back. He may protest to the machine, even swear at it. But it will remain unmoved. He is committed beyond recall. He was committed at the very moment when he put his money into the machine. The contract was concluded at that time. It can be translated into offer and acceptance in this way: the offer is made when the proprietor of the machine holds it out as being ready to receive the money. The acceptance takes place when the customer puts his money into the slot."

The other judges reserved judgment on the precise moment of when the contract was formed but opined that given the seriousness of the condition, more should have been done to draw it to the customer's attention anyway, if the defendants wanted to rely on it.

Analysis: This is an English case but is persuasive authority for the status of automatic vending machines in the timing of conclusion of contracts and, thus, the successful incorporation of terms or otherwise.

Olley v *Marlborough Court Ltd* [1949] 1 KB 532

Court: Court of Appeal (English case)

Issue: Incorporation of express terms into contract when notice placed in hotel bedroom.

Facts: A couple went to a hotel and booked in. They went to their room in which there was a notice saying "The proprietors will not hold themselves responsible for articles lost or stolen, unless handed to the manageress for safe custody. Valuables should be deposited for safe custody in a sealed package and a receipt obtained." Furs, jewellery and other items were stolen from the room, apparently by a young man who had taken the key from the key board on which it hung in reception.

Claim: Mrs Olley claimed against the hotel company for her loss based on its negligence – the hotel had a duty at common law to take reasonable care of the key. It denied negligence but, in any event, argued that there was an exclusion clause in the contract and so even if liability was established, it had been excluded effectively.

Decision: The Court of Appeal found in favour of Mrs Olley. The hotel had been negligent and liability had not been excluded. The notice in the bedroom had not been incorporated into the contract which was made before the notice was seen.

Judgment: Much of the judgment concerns the fundamental issue of liability or otherwise of the hotel for its role in the theft in the first place but there are important statements about the incorporation of the exclusion clause, especially from Lord Denning who is of the opinion at p 549 that "notices put up in bedrooms do not of themselves make a contract. As a rule, the guest does not see them until after he has been accepted as a guest. The hotel company no doubt hope that the guest will be held bound by them, but the hope is vain unless they clearly show that he agreed to be bound by them, which is rarely the case".

Analysis: Another useful case (albeit English) highlighting the importance of identifying when the contract is formed because contractual terms cannot be incorporated thereafter without the consent of the parties.

McWhirter v *Longmuir* 1948 SC 577

Court: Inner House, Court of Session

Issue: Inclusion of *implied* term in contract.

Facts: Under a scheme operating as a result of the Second World War, dairymen were allowed to operate in certain areas to regulate distribution networks of vital supplies of milk. One dairyman transferred his part of a zone to another when he was going on military service. The contract included a price for this and a term that the area should be transferred back to the seller on giving 28 days' written notice and repayment of the purchase price. The contract was also discussed at a meeting of the association which regulated the zones at which the inclusion of a time limit for giving this notice was raised but not included in the contract. The seller was demobilised early and 2 years later had discussions with the purchaser about getting the zone back. He made clear his intentions that he wished to buy it back but he did not give written notice until a few months after that.

Claim: The seller, Mr McWhirter, raised an action to have the contract implemented, arguing that there was no express term in the contract specifying a time period within which written notice had been given and no *implied* term to that effect either as there was no legal authority for implying a term connected with the exercise of a right, rather than discharge of an obligation. The purchaser, Mr Longmuir, argued that the court should hold that the notice had not been given in a reasonable period of time and so should not be implemented: he founded on *Morton* v *Muir* and *The Moorcock*, arguing that business efficacy meant that this should be the case.

Decision: The court found in favour of Mr McWhirter, the seller, and restored the part of the zone to him.

Judgment: Their Lordships held that the contract was to endure as long as the war-time scheme endured and that as consideration of a time limit had been made but not included in a revisal to the contract at a meeting with the association administering the scheme, there was no contractual time limit for serving the notice on parties. The "business efficacy" test would apply, according to Lord Jamieson at p 588: "The Court will only hold a term or condition to be implied in a written contract if its nature is such that it must necessarily be implied to give the contract business efficacy, and in the circumstances under which this contract came into being I think a strong case of necessity would require to be made out." He did not think that it had. Lord Mackay doubted that Morton had been decided on the basis of the *dictum* in *The Moorcock* and noted that *The Moorcock* was specifically decided "for business contracts of [the] type" in that particular case.

Analysis: Scots law allows clauses to be implied to give a contract business efficacy but the aim of the contract has to be taken into account in deciding where that line is drawn.

Lothian v *Jenolite* 1969 SC 111

Court: Inner House, Court of Session

Issue: Inclusion of implied term in contract.

Facts: Jenolite Ltd entered into a contract with Mr Lothian whereby Mr Lothian would sell its goods in Scotland on commission. The contract was to run for 4 years but Jenolite terminated it after 17 months.

Claim: Mr Lothian sued for breach of contract. The company argued that this was a contract of agency and so had an *implied* term that the agent, Mr Lothian, could not sell goods for other businesses without their consent. He had done so and so they were entitled to terminate the contract on the ground of his material breach. The following decision was made at a procedural hearing to determine a reclaiming motion on, *inter alia*, whether there was a breach of contract at all.

Decision: The court held in favour of Mr Lothian.

Judgment: There was no such implied term in a contract of agency (and so no breach). Mr Lothian's argument was that the cases of

Morton and *McWhirter* laid down strict tests in determining when business efficacy applies to allow the inclusion of an implied term and that Gloag had made the point that it is more difficult to imply a term in a written contract than in a verbal one (Lord Milligan at p 120). Lord Milligan said that the test was "formidable" and that the circumstances in which terms will be implied were "rightly very limited". He noted the tests as those laid down in *Morton* and *McWhirter*. In *Morton*, the test was an objective test of the "reasonable man" and in *McWhirter* the test was that the implied term "must necessarily be implied to give the contract business efficacy". The tests were not fulfilled in this case.

Analysis: This case pre-dates the Commercial Agents (Council Directive) Regulations 1993 which govern notice, termination, compensation and indemnification of commercial agents today but is of interest in regard to the reluctance of courts to imply terms on the grounds of reasonableness and business efficacy unless both of these "formidable" tests are fulfilled.

Bank of Scotland v *Dunedin Property Investment Co Ltd (No 1)*
1998 SC 657

Court: Inner House, Court of Session

Issue: Interpretation or construction of contracts.

Facts: The parties entered into an agreement under which Dunedin was permitted to buy stock which was the subject of a loan stock agreement "subject to the bank being fully reimbursed for all costs, charges and expenses incurred by it in connection with the stock". The loan stock agreement had a fixed rate of interest. When Dunedin exercised that right, the matter in dispute was whether those "costs, charges and expenses" included a payment the bank had to make to terminate a swap contract it had entered into with a third party as a hedge against interest fluctuations.

Not surprisingly, Dunedin argued that the swap contract charge incurred by the Bank of Scotland was not incurred "in connection with" its own transaction.

Decision: The Inner House disagreed with Dunedin on a number of grounds.

Judgment: Clearly, the words "in connection with" could be given an ordinary meaning which included this charge and Lord Rodger used this as his starting point. His Lordship did not think it necessary to add the word "*directly*" to "incurred". However, background was also considered and much of the judgment focuses on the question of how far the court can delve into background to make sense of the contract.

Construction in this case was also set in the context of the objective commercial reality of the contract: a fixed rate of interest was realistic only if the bank did enter into a separate hedging agreement and despite the general rule that pre-contractual negotiations cannot be included in the "matrix", discussions between the parties were taken into account to establish their *state of knowledge* at the time the contract was made.

As Lord Rodger said at p 665:

"... the rule which excludes evidence of prior communings as an aid to interpretation of a concluded contract is well established and salutary. The rationale of the rule shows, however, that it has no application when the evidence of the parties' discussions is being considered, not in order to provide a gloss on the terms of the contract, but rather to establish the parties' knowledge of the circumstances with reference to which they used the words in the contract. For that reason I am satisfied that it was proper for the Lord Ordinary to take account of the evidence about what was said at the meeting on 8 June in order to establish the relevant circumstances in which the words of Condition 3 were used."

Analysis: Although reference to pre-contractual negotiations is generally barred when interpreting the meaning of a contract, it may be appropriate to consider them as evidence of the parties' *own* knowledge at the time the contract was made. This is one of the leading Scottish cases on contractual interpretation and should now be read in conjunction with the latest Scottish Supreme Court case on the issue: *Multi-Link* v *North Lanarkshire Council* (below) which in turn has been influenced by the important English case of *Investors Compensation Scheme Ltd* v *West Bromwich Building Society (No 1)* [1998] 1 WLR 896 (also below).

Investors Compensation Scheme Ltd v *West Bromwich Building Society (No 1)* [1998] 1 WLR 896

Court: House of Lords (English case)

Issue: Classic English case on contractual interpretation: how far can the court go in examining the context or factual matrix within which a contract was concluded when asked to interpret its terms?

Facts: The case centres on the interpretation of a compensation scheme for investors under which claims against their building society for losses arising out of certain mortgages were assigned to the Scheme.

Claim: The building society argued that the investors had not assigned their claims to the Scheme and the Scheme argued that they had.

Decision: The claims had been assigned to the Scheme, so claims for damages could be made by the Scheme.

Judgment: Lord Hoffmann delivered a very important judgment and set out at p 912 *et seq* what he called the "common sense principles" by which contracts should be interpreted:

"The principles may be summarised as follows.

(1) Interpretation is the ascertainment of the meaning which the document would convey to a reasonable person having all the background knowledge which would reasonably have been available to the parties in the situation in which they were at the time of the contract.

(2) The background was famously referred to by Lord Wilberforce as the 'matrix of fact', but this phrase is, if anything, an understated description of what the background may include. Subject to the requirement that it should have been reasonably available to the parties and to the exception to be mentioned next, it includes absolutely anything which would have affected the way in which the language of the document would have been understood by a reasonable man.

(3) The law excludes from the admissible background the previous negotiations of the parties and their declarations of subjective intent. They are admissible only in an action for rectification. The law makes this distinction for reasons of

practical policy and, in this respect only, legal interpretation differs from the way we would interpret utterances in ordinary life. The boundaries of this exception are in some respects unclear. But this is not the occasion on which to explore them.

(4) The meaning which a document (or any other utterance) would convey to a reasonable man is not the same thing as the meaning of its words. The meaning of words is a matter of dictionaries and grammars; the meaning of the document is what the parties using those words against the relevant background would reasonably have been understood to mean. The background may not merely enable the reasonable man to choose between the possible meanings of words which are ambiguous but even (as occasionally happens in ordinary life) to conclude that the parties must, for whatever reason, have used the wrong words or syntax: see *Mannai Investments Co. Ltd.* v *Eagle Star Life Assurance Co. Ltd.* [1997] A.C. 749.

(5) The 'rule' that words should be given their 'natural and ordinary meaning' reflects the common sense proposition that we do not easily accept that people have made linguistic mistakes, particularly in formal documents. On the other hand, if one would nevertheless conclude from the background that something must have gone wrong with the language, the law does not require judges to attribute to the parties an intention which they plainly could not have had. Lord Diplock made this point more vigorously when he said in *Antaios Compania Naviera S.A.* v *Salen Rederierna A.B.* [1985] A.C. 191, 201:

'if detailed semantic and syntactical analysis of words in a commercial contract is going to lead to a conclusion that flouts business commonsense, it must be made to yield to business commonsense.'"

Analysis: Lord Hoffmann used this case to develop the "contextual" rather than "literal" approach to contractual interpretation, building on the departure from the "legalistic" approach made in earlier cases. Some of the rules have been clarified further, not least by Lord Hoffmann himself since this decision. *Rainy Sky SA* v *Kookmin Bank* [2011] UKSC 50 reinforces Lord Hoffmann's "common sense principles" in *ICS* as the guiding principles in English law and says that if two meanings are possible, the court should go with the one which makes more commercial sense but noted that Lord Hoffmann clarified Lord Diplock's remark about language in the case of *Co-operative Wholesale Society Ltd* v *National Westminster Bank plc* [1995] 1 EGLR 97 at 98 by adding that:

> "[Lord Diplock's] robust declaration does not mean, however, that one can rewrite the language which the parties have used in order to make the contract conform to business common sense. But language is a very flexible instrument and, if it is capable of more than one construction, one chooses that which seems most likely to give effect to the commercial purpose of the agreement."

This was a controversial decision which appeared to expand the matrix of fact within which the contract should be interpreted very substantially. Although Lord Hoffmann appears to say at one point that any background can be considered, he has himself said that when considering background matter, it is that which the reasonable man would think "relevant" that is important. Nevertheless, this was a clear move away from the literal approach to interpretation in the English courts.

The most decisive Scottish judgment post *ICS* is in *Multi-Link Leisure Developments (Scotland) Ltd* v *North Lanarkshire Council* [2010] UKSC 47, 2011 SC (UKSC) 53 (below).

Multi-Link Leisure Developments (Scotland) Ltd v *North Lanarkshire Council* [2010] UKSC 47, 2011 SC (UKSC) 53

Court: Supreme Court (Scottish case)

Issue: Contractual interpretation.

Facts: In this case, Multi-Link (tenants) and North Lanarkshire Council (landlords) entered into a lease in 2000, which was varied in 2001. The disputed clause said:

> "The price to be paid by Multi-Link [the tenants] in terms of this clause ('the option price') shall, if the option to purchase is exercised within the first year of the period of let, be the sum of ONE HUNDRED AND THIRTY THOUSAND POUNDS (£130,000) STERLING. The option price, if the option to purchase is exercised subsequent to the first year of let, shall be equal to the full market value of the subjects hereby let as at the date of entry for the proposed purchase (as determined

by the landlords) of agricultural land or open space suitable for development as a golf course but, for the avoidance of doubt, shall be not less than the sum of ONE HUNDRED AND THIRTY THOUSAND POUNDS (£130,000) STERLING. In determining the full market value (i) the landlords shall assume (a) that the subjects hereby let are in good and substantial order and repair and that all obligations of the landlords and the tenants under this lease have been complied with, and (b) that the subjects hereby let are ready for occupation, and (ii) the landlords shall disregard (a) any improvements carried out by the tenants during the period of this lease otherwise than in pursuance of an obligation [to] the landlords, and (b) any damage to or destruction of the subjects hereby let."

By clause 18.6 it was provided, for the avoidance of doubt, that the option to purchase was personal to Multi-Link and that it was to be exercisable only so long as they were tenants under the lease.

Between the time that the lease was executed and the exercise of that option by the tenants, there was a change in circumstances surrounding planning law issues. The Structure Plan affecting the area included the leased subjects within three sites zoned for development: in other words, a change of use was on the cards. In 2008, the Local Plan confirmed the area as having potential for housing.

Claim: The dispute was over the valuation of the land to be calculated in terms of the option clause. The tenants argued that the valuation was limited to valuation on the basis of use as a golf course but the landlords argued that it should be full commercial valuation, taking into account its potential for housing which inflated the valuation dramatically.

Decision: The Supreme Court decided in favour of the landlords, the Council.

Judgment: There are two "streams" of construction within the judgment: Lord Hope's and Lord Rodger's.
Lord Hope:

1. Begin with Lord Hoffmann's Rules 1 and 2: words should be given their "ordinary meaning" in the context of the contract, noting at para 11 that:

"Effect is to be given to every word, so far as possible, in the order in which they appear in the clause in question. Words should not be added which are not there, and words which are there should not be changed, taken out or moved from the place in the clause where they have been put by the parties."

2. However, he noted that "[i]t may be necessary to do some of these things at a later stage to make sense of the language. But this should not be done until it has become clear that the language the parties actually used creates an ambiguity which cannot be solved otherwise".

3. Lord Hope then went on to apply Rules 4, 5 and 6 because he did find ambiguity: the two parts of the clause did not marry – they seemed to Lord Hope to be dealing with different issues.

At para 21, Lord Hope said "It has, of course, long been recognised that the commercial or business object of the provision in question may be relevant" and he referred to a number of authorities, including *BoS* v *Dunedin* and *ICS*.

The commercial imperative of the landlords was their statutory duty to get best price for the land. Any other interpretation would give the tenants a "windfall" and Lord Hope concluded that "reasonable commercial men" would have expected the clause to mean that full market value with development potential taken into account should be paid.

Lord Hope therefore started with the ordinary meaning in the contractual context but then moved to putting the whole contract into its commercial context and background to make sense of it.

Lord Rodger:

1. Begin with Rule 1 and specifically those parts which are clear and then use those as a basis for "unravelling" the unclear parts.

2. Requiring the landlords to part with the land on an artificial basis of restricted use "would be a highly unusual and artificial approach to valuation – far less to determining 'the full market value' of the land. Construing Clause 18.2 as a whole and as part of a commercial agreement, I am satisfied that the words in question are not to be interpreted as requiring the landlords to adopt this unusual approach and to ignore the hope value. Had the parties intended the landlords to assume that the land was to be used only as a golf course, I would have expected to find that assumption included among the others at the end of the clause. For these reasons the landlords are entitled to have regard to the hope value of the golf course when assessing its full market value."

Lord Rodger's approach appears therefore to be rooted more firmly in the analysis of language, rather than background: he would have expected to see much more explicit language restricting the valuation to a particular basis for the tenants to win. That said, this is still set in the context of commercial reality, for how else would we know that the tenants' interpretation would be a "highly unusual result"?

Analysis: The Scottish approach to interpretation has taken account of Lord Hoffmann's approach, especially in the reasoning of Lord Hope, but is still rooted in the words themselves. The starting point is the literal interpretation but that is set against the commercial context either to interpret the words themselves (Lord Hope) or as a check that the interpretation is correct (Lord Rodger).

Bank of Nova Scotia v *Hellenic (The Good Luck)* [1992] 1 AC 233

Court: House of Lords (English case)

Issue: Status of warranties in contracts of marine insurance.

Facts: The ship's owner had bought *The Good Luck* with a loan from the Bank which stipulated that the ship should be insured against war risks, that the owners should not do anything to prejudice the insurance and should not take the ship into a war zone without prior notice to the Bank and the insurers. The owners took out insurance which allowed entry to some higher-risk areas on payment of additional premiums but no entry at all to "prohibited zones". The ship went to the Arabian Gulf during the first Gulf War, crossed from an additional premium zone into a prohibited zone and was hit by an Iraqi missile: it was a constructive write-off. The insurers refused to pay out on the ground of breach of warranty: by entering the prohibited zone, the owners were in breach of the promissory warranty not to enter such zones and, as a result, the ship was uninsured at that time.

Claim: The Bank sued the insurers for damages arising as a result of the insurers' failure to tell it that the ship had been in a prohibited zone in terms of agreements between them and that it was uninsured, which the insurers knew. The Bank had advanced more money to the owners at that time and would not have done so if it had been aware of this fact. The insurers argued that their liability had ceased as soon as the owners breached the promissory warranty about entering prohibited zones.

Decision: The House of Lords decided in favour of the Bank on the breach of the contract between them but noted the effect of s 33(3) on the contract of insurance itself.

Judgment: Section 33(3) of the Marine Insurance Act 1906 applied to the contract of insurance itself.

Analysis: This case is included in this section as a reminder that the term "warranty" has a special meaning in contracts of insurance. It does not carry this weight in the general law of contract in Scotland, although the position differs in English contract law.

Abchurch Steamship Co v *Stinnes* 1912 SC 1010, 1911 SLT 72

Court: Inner House, Court of Session

Issue: Interpretation of *ejusdem generis* (lists).

Facts: The contract for the charter of a ship by Mr Stinnes from Abchurch (a shipping contract is known as a "charter party") stated:

> "The vessel is to be loaded in 66 running hours (from 2 P.M. Saturdays to 6 A.M. Mondays, colliery and other holidays excepted unless used). … The time for loading is to commence from the first high-water after arrival in Rhodes, and written notice of readiness, given in ordinary business hours. …Demurrage at the rate of 16s. 8d. per hour to be paid for all detention over the specified time for loading and discharging, accidents, holidays, strikes, lock-outs, or stoppages at the colliery or collieries with which ship is booked to load, or of frost, floods, riots, storms, detention by railway or cranes, stoppage of trains, accidents to machinery or any other unavoidable cause preventing the loading or unloading of the cargo, excepted from hours named for loading and discharging."

(Note: "Demurrage" means the time for which the charterer has the ship before it is loaded and after it is unloaded.)

Mr Stinnes was delayed in loading because there was so much traffic at the port that he could not get the use of the cranes owned by the North British Railway Co to load up until later (these were the only way to load).

Claim: The owners claimed a demurrage charge for the delay and Mr Stinnes argued that it was not payable because it was "detention by cranes" as stipulated in the charter party or, if not, then it fell under the exceptions in the contract which included "any other unavoidable cause preventing the loading or unloading of the cargo".

Decision: The court held in favour of the owners.

Judgment: Much of the judgment focuses on whether the delay was a "detention by cranes" and, ultimately, the court decided that it was simply "want of a berth" and not detention as understood in shipping. On the matter of lists, the Lord President reiterated the rule that the general words such as "any other unavoidable cause" can only be interpreted to include matters, objects etc of the same type as those in the preceding list. The "want of a berth" was not in the same *genus* as the list which contained examples of arrangements which had broken down.

Analysis: This principle can only be used to include a matter, object, thing, ground etc in a list by the addition of words such as "and the like" if there is an identifiable *genus* in the list preceding the general words and the thing in question is in the same *genus*.

THIRD-PARTY RIGHTS

Finnie v *Glasgow and South-Western Railway Co* (1857) 3 Macq 75

Court: House of Lords (Scottish case)

Issue: Did Mr Finnie benefit from a *jus quaesitum tertio* resulting from a contract between two railway companies?

Facts: Mr Finnie argued that he was owed reduced costs for the carriage of coal under a contract between two railway companies. He was not a party to the contract.

Claim: Mr Finnie sought to enforce this third-party right.

Decision: The court did not find that any such right existed.

Judgment: The court made clear that a third-party right must be more than a mere interest in the contract but must have been created for the purpose of benefiting the third party. In this case, the contract did not say who the third party was and, although it was not necessary for the third party to be named, a *"tertius"* or third party would have to be created in it.

Analysis: The creation of a third-party right requires a benefit in favour of the third party and for the third party to be identified, either as an individual or as part of a group, though not necessarily named.

BREACH OF CONTRACT

Lord Elphinstone v *Monkland Iron & Coal Co Ltd* (1866) 13 R (HL) 98

Court: House of Lords

Issue: Penalty clause versus liquidate damages clause.

Facts: A clause in a contract purported to quantify liquidate damages but was based on a one-off sum payable in a range of scenarios and breaches.

Claim: A claim for damages on breach under this clause was challenged as unenforceable.

Decision: The clause was a penalty clause and so could not be enforced.

Judgment: The liquidate damages clause must tie the damages sought to the breach in question – a "catch-all" clause is not likely to be a fair estimate of damages for all kinds of breaches.

Analysis: One-off lump-sum payments triggered by a range of events are less likely to be viewed as liquidate damages clauses and more likely to be penalty clauses. This reasoning was also approved in the case of *Dunlop Pneumatic Tyre Co* v *New Garage & Motor Co Ltd* [1915] AC 79 (HL).

Dingwall v *Burnett* 1912 SC 1097

Court: Inner House, Court of Session

Issue: Enforceability of a penalty clause on breach of contract.

Facts: Mr Burnett owned a hotel and entered into an agreement with Mr Dingwall to lease it to him on the condition that the pursuer obtained the hotel licence which at that point was in Mr Dingwall's name. The licence could be transferred only at certain times of the year and so, until then, the pursuer, Mr Dingwall, was to manage the hotel on behalf of the defender, Mr Burnett, and if the licence was not transferred, the agreement would end. The contract contained a clause which stated: "Fifth. Both parties hereto bind and oblige themselves to implement their part of this agreement under the penalty of fifty pounds, to be paid by the party failing to the party performing or willing to perform over and above performance." Mr Dingwall decided not to pursue the lease arrangement once he found out what the turnover of the hotel actually was.

Claim: Mr Dingwall sued for the return of a deposit receipt for £200 which had been lodged to cover furniture etc when he was still intending to take over the licence and tenancy plus unpaid wages as manager. Mr Burnett refused and claimed £250 as damages for breach of contract.

Decision: The court held in favour of Mr Dingwall.

Judgment: The interpretation of the clause dealing with the £50 payment had to be construed within the body of the contract and there was no suggestion that it was meant as a liquidate damages clause and a fair estimate of likely losses in the event of breach, which is the test for enforceability of such clauses. Penalty clauses are not enforceable: liquidate damages clauses are enforceable. The use of the word "penalty" itself was not conclusive but the phrase "over and above performance" suggested that the clause was indeed punitive – additional to and not instead of performance. Lord Salvesen (with whom the Lord Justice-Clerk and Lord Guthrie concurred) went on to say at p 94 that "An even more important consideration in determining whether the sum stipulated to be paid in the event of a breach of contract is liquidate damages or merely represents a penalty, is to ascertain whether the sum conditioned to be paid bears (in the words of Lord Justice-Clerk Inglis in *Craig*, 1 M. 1020) 'a clear proportion to the amount of loss sustained by the party entitled to claim it'; and very similar language was used by some of the noble Lords who decided the case of *Elphinstone* (13 R (H.L.) 98)."

Analysis: In the words of Lord Salvesen himself, this case does not lay down new law. It simply confirms that a *penalty* clause is not enforceable and does not limit the amount of damages which can be claimed for in the event of breach. By contrast, a properly constructed *liquidate damages* clause can do so.

Clydebank Engineering and Shipbuilding v *Castaneda*
(1904) 7 F (HL) 77

Court: House of Lords (Scottish case)

Issue: Penalty clause or liquidate damages?

Facts: The contract between Clydebank and the Spanish Government for four boats contained a clause awarding the Spanish Government £500 per week per boat in the event of late delivery.

Claim: The boats were very late and the Spanish Government sought to enforce that clause.

Decision: The court decided that the clause was indeed enforceable.

Judgment: The actual damages would have been very difficult and complex to ascertain in this case and so the sum agreed upon of £500 per week was suitable and not simply included to hold over Clydebank's head *"in terrorum"*. It had been negotiated by the parties in the context of this contract where time was of the essence.

Analysis: The use of liquidate damages clauses should be based on estimates of actual damages as agreed between the parties.

Graham & Co v United Turkey Red Co 1922 SC 533

Court: Inner House, Court of Session

Issue: Enforcing a contract when in breach – the mutuality principle.

Facts: Alexander Graham of Graham & Co was a commercial agent and contracted with United Turkey to sell its goods. The contract prohibited the agent from selling goods for others. Mr Graham breached the contract by selling for others and on his own account and then terminated the contract.

Claim: Mr Graham claimed for monies owed up until the point of termination of the contract. United Turkey claimed that it did not have to pay because the agent had been in breach of contract.

Decision: The Court of Session decided that the agent was not entitled to sue on contract for sums due during the period for which the agent was in breach of contract but could obtain an accounting for the period during which he was in breach on another basis.

Judgment: Lord Anderson in the Outer House had argued that only breaches which went to the "root and substance of the contract" had the effect of debarring the party in breach from suing on the contract. In his opinion, Mr Graham had sold goods on its behalf and that was the commission sued for: his breach was on another part of the contract which did not go to the root of it. His Lordship went on to find that the "fundamental purpose" of the contract was for the agent to sell the defenders' goods, which he did. However, by the time this got to appeal, the nature of the breach had been accepted as material by both parties and so the decision was different (much to the chagrin of Lord Salvesen, who noted that much of the action could have been avoided if the facts had been agreed in the first place!).

Analysis: A party in material breach cannot sue on the contract to enforce it. That party may have alterative grounds on which to sue, such as unjustified enrichment, but the mutuality principle means that a breach of contract action is not open to a party in material breach of the contract.

Wade v *Waldon* 1909 SC 571

Court: Inner House, Court of Session

Issue: In the case of breach, can the "innocent party" rescind the contract?

Facts: Mr Wade was booked to perform at the theatre and the contract was subject to conditions on the back, one of which was that "all artistes engaged … must give fourteen days' notice prior to such engagement, such notice to be accompanied with bill matter". Mr Wade did not give the requisite notice and so was not allowed to perform. He had been due to receive £350 per week for the booking.

Claim: Mr Wade claimed £300 for breach of contract. His argument was that the need to give notice was not material to the contract. Mr Wade was well known and never gave notice. Mr Waldon and others then raised actions claiming that Mr Wade was in breach of contract for failing to give notice.

Decision: The decision was in favour of Mr Wade, the performer. The breach did not warrant rescission.

Judgment: The Lord President, at p 576, laid down this statement:

> "It is familiar law, and quite well settled by decision, that in any contract which contains multifarious stipulations there are some which go so to the root of the contract that a breach of those stipulations entitles the party pleading the breach to declare that the contract is at an end. There are others which do not go to the root of the contract, but which are part of the contract, and which would give rise, if broken, to an action of

damages. I need not cite authority upon what is trite and very well settled law."

In this case, it was held that the condition to give notice did not go to the root of the contract.

Analysis: A material breach will entitle the innocent party to rescind but that party has to be careful about classifying the breach as material. If wrong, the rescission is not justified and puts that party in breach himself.

White & Carter (Councils) Ltd v *McGregor* 1962 SC (HL) 1

Court: House of Lords (Scottish case)

Issue: Can one party continue with a contract even if the other gives notice of repudiation?

Facts: Two businesses entered into a contract whereby one, the advertising contractors, would put adverts for the other (a garage business) on to bins for a period of 3 years. The garage owner repudiated the contract on the day it was made, by letter purporting to cancel it, but the advertising contractors decided to go ahead and fulfil their part of it anyway.

Claim: The advertising contractors sued for the whole contract price, on the basis of cl 8 within it which said:

> "In the event of an instalment or part thereof being due for payment, and remaining unpaid for a period of four weeks or in the event of the advertiser being in any way in breach of this contract then the whole amount due for the one hundred and fifty-six weeks or such part of the said one hundred and fifty-six weeks as the advertiser shall not yet have paid shall immediately become due and payable."

The garage owner refused to pay, on the basis that the contract had been "cancelled".

Decision: The advertising contractors' claim won. They did not have to accept the garage's repudiation and damages but could proceed regardless.

Judgment: Lord Reid said at pp 11–12:

> "The general rule cannot be in doubt. It was settled in Scotland at least as early as 1848, and it has been authoritatively stated

time and again in both Scotland and England. If one party to a contract repudiates it in the sense of making it clear to the other party that he refuses or will refuse to carry out his part of the contract, the other party, the innocent party, has an option. He may accept that repudiation and sue for damages for breach of contract, whether or not the time for performance has come; or he may, if he chooses, disregard or refuse to accept it and then the contract remains in full effect."

Analysis: Repudiation does not have to be accepted but do bear in mind Lord Reid's observation that if there was no financial gain to be made from proceeding, then the innocent party might not have this choice so again, a judgment call has to be made before doing this.

Hadley v *Baxendale* 156 ER 145, (1854) 9 Ex 341

Court: House of Lords (English case)

Issue: The test for remoteness of damage.

Facts: The plaintiffs owned a flour mill. The crank shaft of the steam engine which drove the mill broke. They had the broken shaft taken to the defendants, who were carriers (trading as Pickfords), to take it to the works of W Joyce & Co where a new one could be made, using the broken one as a pattern. However, there was an unreasonable delay in having the broken shaft delivered and the mill was closed for several days since it could not operate without this vital piece of equipment.

Claim: The mill owners sued the carriers for the loss of profits that they said arose directly as a result of the delay.

Decision: The court held in favour of the carriers and demanded a new proof.

Judgment: The judgment gives the court at the proof direction to give to the jury in determining the damages. Alderson B gave the famous judgment which stated that the damages for breach of contract should be either those arising "naturally i.e. according to the natural course of things" or damages which might "reasonably be supposed to be in the contemplation of both parties at the time the contract was made". His Lordship went on to name the second category "special circumstances". In this case, all that was shown was that the carriers were told that the shaft was broken and the plaintiffs were mill owners. The carriers were not told that the mill had to stop production as a result. In the "great multitude of cases" in which shafts were sent off, no such consequences would have flowed as there would be spare shafts etc, so the losses did not arise naturally and neither were there special circumstances known to the carriers or in their contemplation.

Analysis: This case is an English one but has formed the basis for the development of the test for measuring remoteness of damages in England and Scotland. The cases below show how the law has developed in each jurisdiction. Note: the court summary for *Hadley* is wrong in that it suggests that the carriers knew that the delivery was urgent. As the court in *Victoria Laundry* noted, all that the carriers knew was that the shaft was broken and the owners had a mill (these facts are the only knowledge imputed to the carriers by the judge in *Hadley*). Be careful about rubrics/court summaries and headers – read the case itself!

Victoria Laundry (Windsor) Ltd v *Newman Industries Ltd*
[1949] 2 KB 528

Court: Court of Appeal (English case)

Issue: Further refinement of the tests in *Hadley* v *Baxendale*.

Facts: Victoria Laundry contracted with Newman Industries to buy and have installed a new larger boiler for its laundry to be able to take on bigger laundry contracts. In a letter to Newman, Victoria Laundry wrote that it intended to "put it into use in the shortest possible space of time". The boiler was delayed by several months because it was damaged by contractors of Newman's and was not installed until November, having been promised in June.

Claim: Victoria Laundry sued for breach of contract, including a claim for loss of profits which would have arisen had the boiler been installed when expected. This totalled £16 per week for 20 weeks for lost business contemplated by its planned expansion and £262 per week for loss of Ministry of Supply contracts on which it missed out.

Decision: The court decided that some profits could be claimed for, but not all. The loss of profits from the planned expansion could be included but not the Government contracts.

Judgment: Lord Asquith noted that the lower court had found loss of profits too remote altogether and awarded no damages under either head. However, in breaking down the judgment in *Hadley,* his Lordship noted that two rules on what was "reasonably foreseeable" had been laid down, each depending on "knowledge possessed". These were: (1) circumstances which are known "in the ordinary course of things" (whether actually known or not – ie they can be imputed); and (2) special circumstances *actually known* by the parties at the time the contract was made. It was, the court found, appropriate to think that the boiler company would know in the ordinary course of things that a laundry which ordered a 19-foot-high boiler costing over £2,000 (a huge sum in those days) would need it for its business (the boiler company knew what Victoria Laundry's business was) and would know more about the uses of boilers than the layman. Thus a loss of business arising out of the delay would be within its imputed knowledge. However, the court could not impute the knowledge about the Government contracts. Those were special circumstances that would have to be actually known about to fall under the second test since that could not fall under the first test.

Analysis: A further breakdown of the two tests set out in *Hadley* – the first test is based on matters known "in the ordinary course of things" and this can include imputed knowledge. However, the second test of special circumstances requires actual knowledge.

Balfour Beatty Construction (Scotland) Ltd v *Scottish Power plc*
[1994] UKHL 11

Court: House of Lords (Scottish case)

Issue: Test for remoteness of damage in breach of contract.

Facts: The facts of this case are relatively straightforward. Balfour Beatty Construction (Scotland) Ltd ("Balfour Beatty") was contracted to build part of the Edinburgh City Bypass in 1985. This work required large quantities of concrete so it set up a concrete batching plant off site and contracted Scottish Power plc (then South of Scotland Electricity Board or "SSEB") to supply the electricity to that plant. The concrete was mixed at the plant and taken by lorries in batches to the site. This system worked well until there was a breakdown in the electricity supply during operations late one day. The breakdown came part of the way through the job to build an aqueduct taking the Union Canal over the road. The construction of the aqueduct required a continuous pour of concrete to ensure the strength of the structure: in other words, concrete arrived from the plant in batches in lorries one after the other and had to be poured into the structure with no more than 30 minutes between pours to avoid weakness caused by one layer of concrete hardening before the next one arrived. Although almost 90 per cent of the concrete was poured, the remaining 10 per cent or so did not arrive because of the power cut. This meant that there was not enough concrete to finish the job in a "continuous pour".

Claim: Balfour Beatty claimed that the breakdown in electricity supply was a breach of contract which caused the job to be defective in that the continuous pour was interrupted, the concrete hardened between layers and the aqueduct had to be demolished and rebuilt. It claimed for the full cost of this: it established breach of contract when the case came to the Outer House of the Court of Session but not the claim for damages. It appealed to the Inner House and won but Scottish Power appealed to the House of Lords.

Decision: The House of Lords upheld Scottish Power's appeal and decided that although there had been a breach of contract when the electricity supply was halted, the loss was too remote and could not be claimed.

Judgment: The judgment was unanimous among the five Law Lords. It was delivered by Lord Jauncey of Tullichettle who made the following key points:

1. The test for remoteness fell to be decided by the tests set out in *Hadley* v *Baxendale* (1854) 9 Exch. 341 (as developed in subsequent case law) and in particular on the interpretation of this passage in relation to the facts of this case:

   "Where two parties have made a contract which one of them has broken, the damages which the other party ought to receive in respect of such breach of contract should be such as may fairly and reasonably be considered either arising naturally, *i.e.*, according to the usual course of things, from such breach of contract itself, or such as may reasonably be supposed to have been in the contemplation of both parties, at the time they made the contract, as the probable result of the breach of it."

2. Applying this law to the facts, the court had to decide what was in the "reasonable contemplation" of SSEB at the time the contract was made.

3. The House of Lords did not think that it was in the "reasonable

contemplation" of SSEB that a continuous pour would be required: this was technical knowledge that, as suppliers, they would not have and neither could they be expected to have.

4. Lord Jauncey found that "It must always be a question of circumstances what one contracting party is presumed to know about the business activities of the other. No doubt the simpler the activity of the one, the more readily can it be inferred that the other would have reasonable knowledge thereof. However, when the activity of A involves complicated construction or manufacturing techniques, I see no reason why who supplies a commodity that A intends to use in the course of those techniques should be assumed, merely because of the order for the commodity, to be aware of the details of all the techniques undertaken by A and the effect thereupon of any failure of or deficiency in that commodity. Even if the [the lower court] had made a positive finding that continuous pour was a regular part of industrial practice it would not follow that in the absence of any other evidence suppliers of electricity such as the Board should have been aware of that practice."

Analysis: This is the leading Scottish case on remoteness of damage and confirms that the interpretation of "reasonable contemplation" must be a question of fact in each individual case.

Transfield Shipping Inc v *Mercator Shipping Inc (The Achilleas)*
[2008] UKHL 48

Court: House of Lords (English case)

Issue: Quantification of damages – what is reasonably foreseeable and in the "ordinary course of things".

Facts: A ship (*The Achilleas*) was chartered (hired out to) Transfield Shipping Inc by its owners on the basis that it would be returned by 2 May. The owners then entered into another charter (shipping term for "hire contract") with a third party, to follow on from the first. The market rate had risen by the time this second contract was made and so that contract was for $39,500 per day but the second charterers could cancel if the ship was not available by 8 May. Transfield were delayed in getting the ship back to the owners and a new date of 11 May was agreed for the second charter. In the course of negotiations, a new daily rate of $31,500 was agreed which reflected a drop in market rates.

Claim: The owners claimed against Transfield for over $1 million, being the difference in daily rates for the 191-day charter which followed on (ie 191 days x $8,000 drop in daily market rates). The case went to arbitration and an arbitration award of this amount was made on the basis that it was a loss naturally arising out of the breach – it was within the ordinary course of things to assume that later re-delivery could compromise a follow-on charter. Transfield appealed to the House of Lords and argued that they should only have to pay the difference in the daily rates for the overrun period (ie the period when the ship was, admittedly, late). In that case, they were paying around $16,000 a day and the market rate was more than double that during the overrun period. However, the second charter had not been intimated to them, and so it was not reasonably foreseeable that the larger 191-day loss would occur.

Decision: The House of Lords decided in favour of Transfield.

Judgment: The judgments in this case focus on remoteness and each of the Law Lords gives an opinion. Lord Hoffmann argued at p 15 that before loss can be quantified, the court has to decide whether the loss is of a kind "for which the contract-breaker ought fairly to be taken to have accepted responsibility". This has its basis in the classification of contracts as voluntary obligations and so the objective intention of the parties has to be ascertained. The reasonable foreseeability of consequences has to be tempered with an understanding of the responsibilities the parties can be assumed to have taken on. At p 22, his Lordship says: "In my opinion, the only rational basis for the distinction is that it reflects what would reasonably have been regarded by the contracting party as significant for the purposes of the risk he was undertaking." The case of *Victoria Laundry* distinguished between two types of loss of profits and here, too, there was a distinction between assuming responsibility for the costs of the delay itself and the costs flowing from the terms of a second charter, the terms of which were unquantifiable and, indeed, unknowable by the parties at the time their contract was made.

Lord Rodger of Earlsferry confirmed that *Hadley v Baxendale* was the starting point for calculating damages and that the two tests were the losses arising in the ordinary course of things and "special circumstances". The second test of "special circumstances" did not arise here: the second charter party was not made known to Transfield when the contract was made. Lord Rodger highlighted the phrase regarding the "ordinary course of things" used by

Alderson J in his judgment which was the result which would flow from the "great multitude of cases" and so, in this case, the norm would have been for the market to fill the gap if the delayed return had a knock-on effect on a follow-on charter. A third charter could reasonably be expected, unless there were other circumstances such as the event occurring at a time of year when bad weather affected the market etc.

Lord Hope was of the opinion at p 31 that "Assumption of responsibility, which forms the basis of the law of remoteness of damage in contract, is determined by more than what at the time of the contract was reasonably foreseeable".

Lord Walker noted that businessmen would have a shared understanding of what was to be expected from the contract.

Analysis: This is an important case because it develops (or perhaps drills deeper) into the test of "ordinary course of things" beyond what is merely reasonably foreseeable to limit it to what the parties can objectively be found to have assumed responsibility for. This ties remoteness back to the fundamental principle of contract law, namely the voluntary nature of the obligations. As an objective test, however, it is not a "'get out of jail' free card" for contract breakers.

Ruxley Electronics and Construction Ltd v *Forsyth* [1996] AC 344

Court: House of Lords (English case)

Issue: Quantification of loss where there is loss of amenity but no patrimonial loss.

Facts: Mr Forsyth contracted with Ruxley to have a swimming pool built at his home, with a deep end of 7 feet, 6 inches. The pool was completed but found to have a deep end of only 6 feet. It was still useable and was not devalued by this fact but not as much "fun", according to Mr Forsyth (p 363). He refused to pay the full price.

Claim: Mr Forysth was sued for the contract price and counter-claimed with an action for damages for defective performance of contract, arguing that he should be entitled to the cost of rebuilding the pool to the agreed specification (£21,650). This had been rejected by the trial judge but overturned by the Court of Appeal.

Decision: The House of Lords agreed with the trial judge – the claim for the full reinstatement cost was unreasonable and an award of £2,500 for loss of amenity was awarded to Mr Forsyth.

Judgment: Lord Bridge of Harwich reiterated at p 353 that damages are not about punishing the party in breach and in his last judicial speech (as he retired thereafter) was pleased to see that in this case "common sense and the common law here go hand in hand": Mr Forsyth should not get both the useable pool and the cost of rebuilding it but should receive damages for a loss of amenity. Both Lord Bridge and Lord Jauncey of Tullichettle reiterated that the amount of damages to be awarded is a question of fact. The usual remedy in defective building contracts is to calculate the reconstruction costs required to put the building right but this is qualified by the need for proportionality and whether reconstruction is reasonable in the circumstances. In this case, there was no difference in value between a pool with a slightly deeper diving area than another and, as Lord Lloyd of Berwick noted, damages must reflect true loss.

Analysis: Defective performance in building contracts is common and the first argument would usually be that damages equate to the amount of money required to put the building works right. However, this is tempered by the principle which underpins damages, ie that damages should reflect the true loss, and so in cases where there is no (or perhaps only minor) patrimonial loss, the court also needs to consider what is reasonable and proportionate. This English case was applied in the Scottish case of *Mclaren Murdoch & Hamilton* v *Abercromby Motor Group Ltd* (see below) and in the English House of Lords case of *Farley* v *Skinner*.

Mclaren Murdoch & Hamilton v *Abercromby Motor Group Ltd*
2003 SCLR 323, 100 Con LR 63, 2002 GWD 38–1242

Court: Outer House, Court of Session

Issue: Defective performance of building contract and potential "legal black hole".

Facts: Architects and a garage owner entered into a contract to design and build a garage showroom which Abercromby later sold on. Abercromby was not happy with the heating system installed, which was not very effective.

Claim: Mclaren sued for the contract price and Abercromby counter-sued with a claim for the reconstruction costs of replacing the heating system to the standard that had been agreed.

Decision: The court held that Abercromby was only entitled to a sum for loss of amenity.

Judgment: Lord Drummond Young considered that Ruxley allowed two exceptions to the general rule that a pursuer's claim for damages in building contacts should amount to what is required to make the project conform to the contract: first, where such a cost would be manifestly disproportionate to any benefit gained by the pursuer; and, second, where the defender can lead evidence that it would be disproportionate.

His Lordship also held that the fact that Abercromby had sold on the garage did not create a "legal back hole" in which no party has title and interest to sue on a contract. Abercromby was not the owner of the garage at the time of the court action but did have title to sue because the defect arose on construction, not on discovery, and so Abercromby was owner at the relevant time and had title to sue. Had his Lordship decided otherwise, then neither Abercromby nor the new owner would have been able to sue. Abercromby would have lost the right since the loss would not have been its right: it no longer owned the building and the new owner would not have had any right to sue for defective performance of the contract because it was not party to the contract.

Analysis: In calculating damages for defective performance of building contracts, be aware of the proportionality factor. Building contracts are such that to remedy a defect, massive building works may have to be undertaken and if the benefit to the pursuer is such that it cannot be justified then the courts will take that on board. Be careful not to assume that this exception applies to all contracts and that, even in building contracts, this is a matter of degree.

Addis v *Gramophone* [1909] AC 488

Court: House of Lords (English case)

Issue: Limitation of damages in cases where loss is non-patrimonial.

Facts: A man was dismissed from his employment and it was established that the dismissal was a breach of contract.

Claim: The wronged employee sued for £600 – a sum which the House of Lords noted must surely have been overtaken by the costs of taking this case all the way there! Part of that claim was for injured feelings at the way in which the dismissal had been carried out.

Decision: The House awarded the dismissed employee £340 for lost salary and commission but nothing for injured feelings.

Judgment: The manner of the dismissal (abrupt and oppressive) had no bearing on the amount of damages claimed. The amount should be in relation to lost salary and not for injured feelings.

Analysis: This case sets out the general rule that damages cover only patrimonial loss but there have been developments in this area, as set out in the cases below.

Jarvis v *Swans Tours* [1973] QB 233

Court: Court of Appeal (English case)

Issue: Damages for disappointing holiday.

Facts: A solicitor, Mr Jarvis, booked a "house-party-style" skiing holiday which was advertised in glowing terms in a brochure but it failed to live up to advertised expectations and was very disappointing. In the first week, there were hardly any guests at the house party and, in the second week, none at all. Promised food, skiing and entertainment failed to materialise.

Claim: Mr Jarvis claimed for breach of contract and general damages for loss of benefit and inconvenience and special damages of (a) his salary for the 2 weeks he was on holiday, even although he had been paid because he had used up his paid entitlement but had not benefited from a good holiday; and (b) the cost of the holiday itself.

Decision: The Court of Appeal found in his favour and awarded £125.

Judgment: Lord Denning held at pp 237 and 238 that there were exceptions to the general rule that damages could not be claimed for distress: "In a proper case damages for mental distress can be recovered in contract, just as damages for shock can be recovered in tort. One such case is a contract for a holiday, or any other contract to provide entertainment and enjoyment. If the contracting party breaks his contract, damages can be given for the disappointment, the distress, the upset and frustration caused by the breach."

Analysis: This English case is an exception to the general limitation on claiming damages for mental distress but the nature of contracts where damages for disappointment etc can be claimed are very limited. A Scottish example is found in *Diesen* v *Samson* below.

Diesen v *Samson* 1971 SLT (Sh Ct) 48

Court: Sheriff court

Issue: Scottish case of damages for mental distress.

Facts: A bride booked a photographer to take photos of her wedding but he breached the contract by failing to turn up and so the only photo that the couple had of their wedding was one of them outside the church which happened to be taken by a newspaper covering the story of the groom's Norwegian national dress. Nowadays, of course, the bride would have thousands of photos available from mobile phones!

Claim: The bride claimed for mental distress.

Decision: The bride was awarded damages for mental distress.

Judgment: The sheriff-substitute identified the key issue as being whether the court could award damages for injury to feelings and noted that the case of *Addis* appeared also to reflect the law of Scotland since it was cited as an authority by Gloag and other writers. It was noted in the judgment that his Lordship could therefore consider English textbooks and found a passage on exceptions to the rule. The sheriff-substitute identified this non-commercial contract as falling within the exceptions.

Analysis: English and Scots law appear to be the same here – certain limited types of contracts (holidays, weddings, contracts for enjoyment) can lead to damages for mental distress if breached. Quantification of damages – ie working out how much to award – remains tricky.

Farley v *Skinner* [2002] 2 AC 732

Court: House of Lords (English case)

Issue: Non-pecuniary loss in a house purchase.

Facts: Mr Farley wanted to buy a house and contracted with a surveyor to give him a valuation. He made it clear that he did not want to buy a house which was affected by too much aircraft noise from Gatwick Airport which was a few miles away. The surveyor valued the property correctly but was negligent in advising his client that the house would not be substantially affected by noise from aircraft. In fact, when Mr Farley moved in, he found that it was adversely affected by the flight path. He had bought it as a retirement property, though, and decided not to move there.

Claim: The client sued the surveyor for breach of contract and sought damages for loss of amenity. There was no financial loss because the house had been correctly valued but was not the peaceful retreat it was meant to be.

Decision: The House of Lords agreed with the trial judge and awarded £10,000 for loss of amenity. This amount was considered to be at the uppermost limit of what could be expected in this kind of case.

Judgment: This house purchase did fall into the category of exceptions to the general rule that damages cannot be awarded for mental distress, loss of amenity etc. It was bought as a peaceful retreat in retirement and the law recognises that contracts which have as their *object* the intention to give peace of mind, relaxation etc are in a different class from other contracts and so damages should be payable in those cases.

Analysis: In this case, the purpose of buying the house was important as it took it from a mere house purchase into the category of exceptions to the general rule about damages for mental distress. The court examined the "very object" of the contract before concluding that it was one of the exceptions.

Gunter & Co v *Lauritzen* 1894 1 SLT 435

Court: Outer House, Court of Session

Issue: Is there a duty to mitigate losses on the part of the innocent party in cases of breach of contract?

Facts: Lauritzen sold Danish hay to Gunter & Co who were going to re-sell it on delivery. Lauritzen knew about the re-sale. The hay which he delivered was not conform to contract and the purchasers lost out on their re-sale profit.

Claim: Gunter & Co sued for damages and the defender argued that they should have mitigated their loss on the re-sale contract by buying more hay on the open market and protecting their profit that way.

Decision: The court decided in favour of Gunter & Co, the purchasers.

Judgment: There was no open market for Dutch hay in the place of delivery (Aberdeen) and so no duty to take extraordinary steps to secure new supplies in this case but it seems to suggest that otherwise there would be.

Analysis: Although this case appears to suggest that there is a duty to mitigate, Professor McBryde has cast doubt on whether there is an *actual* duty to do so in Scots law (see McBryde on *Contract* (2007), para 22-37).

Experience Hendrix LLC v *PPX Enterprises Inc*
[2003] 1 All ER (Comm) 830

Court: Court of Appeal (English case)

Issue: Gains-based damages. How to assess damages where the wrongdoer has profited from the breach but the claimant has not suffered any pecuniary loss.

Facts: The estate of the late Jimi Hendrix entered into a settlement agreement with one party about the grant of licences to recordings by the musician. Licences appeared to have been given to third parties of recordings not included in the head agreement.

Claim: The estate (through the company called Experience Hendrix LLC) sued for damages based on clawing back the profits made as a result of the breach.

Decision: The Court of Appeal held that this case did not fall into the very limited exception to the general rule that damages could not include an accounting of profits

Judgment: The exception to the rule that restitutionary damages or gains-based damages are not competent can be found in the case of *Attorney General* v *Blake* [2001] 1 AC 268 in which a former spy had to account for profits from breaching a contractual obligation to HM Government not to disclose secrets. It is clearly a very limited category and, in this case, the breach of contract occurred in a commercial setting and so the usual rules of damages should apply.

Analysis: Gains-based damages will be awarded only in very rare circumstances and the fact that a breach occurs in a commercial setting may render that even more unlikely.

TERMINATION OF CONTRACT

Taylor v *Caldwell* (1863) 122 ER 309

Court: King's Bench (English case)

Issue: *Rei interitus* and frustration of contract by destruction of its subject-matter.

Facts: A concert hall was to be hired for a series of concerts but was destroyed by fire beforehand. The contract did not provide for this event but the plaintiffs who had hired the venue had lost out on profits etc as a result.

Claim: The plaintiffs claimed for damages arising out of breach of contract.

Decision: The court held that the contract could not be fulfilled and damages were not payable.

Judgment: Following discussion of civil law and English law, the court concluded: "The principle seems to us to be that, in contracts in which the performance depends on the continued existence of a given person or thing, a condition is implied that the impossibility of performance arising from the perishing of the person or thing shall excuse the performance."

Analysis: This contract was frustrated by the destruction of the subject-matter without fault on the part of either side but many contracts today would include a contractual remedy on what should happen in these circumstances.

Mackeson v *Boyd* 1942 SC 56

Court: Inner House, Court of Session

Issue: Frustration of contract – constructive destruction of the subject-matter of the contract.

Facts: Mr Boyd contracted to lease a furnished mansion to a tenant and his successors but the property was requisitioned for troops during the Second World War after the tenant's heir, Mrs Mackeson, had inherited the lease and moved in. The landlord refused to allow

Mrs Mackeson to abandon the lease.

Claim: Mrs Mackeson sought declarator that the lease was no longer binding as a result of the requisition.

Decision: The court found in favour of Mrs Mackeson.

Judgment: The court found that there had been *rei interitus* resulting from the requisition and so the lease was frustrated.

Analysis: The case was based on *Tay Salmon Fisheries Co* v *Speedie* in which there was also "notional" rather than "actual" destruction. The court did not think that the ground for the decision here was eviction, because eviction is based on breach of warranty which did not arise, but rather on the principle of *rei interitus*.

Fraser & Co Ltd v *Denny, Mott & Dickson Ltd* 1944 SC (HL) 35

Court: House of Lords (Scottish case)

Issue: Frustration of contract by outbreak of war.

Facts: There was an option to purchase subjects contained in an agreement relating to a timber yard which could be exercised on termination of the lease by either party. The lease itself was brought to an end when it was rendered illegal by war-time rules on the control of timber (supervening illegality). The appellants wanted to exercise the option to purchase and sent notice of termination and exercise of option to the owners.

Claim: The appellants claimed that the option to purchase was still enforceable.

Decision: The House of Lords held in favour of the owners – the option to purchase had lapsed with the supervening illegality which frustrated the contract.

Judgment: Lord Maclaren gives a detailed account of the development of the jurisprudence here, noting that the law of England and Scotland are the same. The option to purchase was dependent on one or other party terminating the contract but by the time notice was served, the contract had already been terminated by a supervening illegality – "you cannot slay the slain".

Analysis: A good example of events overtaking the parties. Although there may be merit in some of the argument about whether parts of the contract were severable, the facts here did not support such an argument because of the wording of the option but, in other circumstances, only part of a contract might be struck at by a supervening illegality so we should not assume that the whole contract is necessarily frustrated.

Krell v *Henry* [1903] 2 KB 740

Court: Court of Appeal (English case)

Issue: Frustration by supervening event.

Facts: Mr Henry hired from Mr Krell a flat on Pall Mall in London for the two days on which the Coronation of the new King was due to take place, so that Mr Henry and his party could watch the Coronation procession which was due to take that route. The King became ill and the Coronation had to be re-arranged. Mr Henry wanted to cancel the contract but Mr Krell insisted on payment. The contract did not state the purpose of the rental, although the two days were clearly related to the Coronation and the advert for the flat had referred to its location in relation to the Coronation procession.

Claim: Mr Krell sued for the contract price.

Decision: The court found in favour of Mr Henry and no further rental monies were due beyond the deposit.

Judgment: *Taylor* v *Caldwell* was applied here. The contract had been frustrated by a supervening event. Although not express, it was implied in the terms of the agreement that the foundation of it was the Coronation and, that having been cancelled, it frustrated the contract.

Analysis: The circumstances are highly unusual here and a leading text on English contract law, *Chitty on Contract*, says at para 23-034 that the decision has been criticised and is highly unlikely to be extended. The writer notes the fact that the rental was for the days only, and not the nights, was probably "a deciding factor" to link it to the Coronation so completely.